roomrecipes

roomrecipes

Ingredients for Great-Looking Rooms

Cheryl and Jeffrey Katz

ROCKPORT PUBLISHERS

Still life photographs by Hornick/Rivlin

First published in the United States of America by
Rockport Publishers, Inc.
33 Commercial Street
Gloucester, Massachusetts 01930-5089
Telephone: (978) 282-9590
Facsimile: (978) 283-2742

www.rockpub.com

ISBN 1-56496-694-1

10 9 8 7 6 5 4 3 2

Design: Moore Moscowitz
Cover Photography: Hornick/Rivlin
Layout and Production: Terry Patton Rhoads

Printed in China

contents

introduction

There is a magical moment when you visit a house for the first time and enter a particular room that triggers a treasured remembrance—a bedroom shared with a younger sister, a supper in the kitchen, a secret hiding spot, the vibrant colors in a painting by a favorite artist. That room even makes us remember intangible things like the comfort of a favorite reading chair, the coolness of a lake on a hot summer day. Inevitably, these are the rooms that we like best, that we remember long after our visit.

This book is about making rooms that capture those moments, while considering the things that meet the needs of our day to day lives. We want rooms that function well. We want elegant rooms for quiet conversation. We want comfortable rooms to watch a movie with friends. We want warm cozy rooms where we can hide from the world. We want rooms that represent our past, yet include all the comforts of the present, and are ready for the future. We want rooms that are spiritual or frivolous or just beautiful.

Often we know how our rooms should "feel" but we don't always know how to translate that feeling into reality. How do we make rooms that are right for us?

Linger in a room and begin to focus on each detail. Start with the color of the walls. Is the color deep? Is the woodwork white—or does it match the wall color? Think about the materials. If there is metal in the room is it polished nickel? Antique brass? Is the floor carpeted? Or is it wood? Is it pale wide plank pine? Or dark mahogany? Are there moldings? Are they ornate or modern? Is the room flooded with light? Is the drapery richly textured? Are the fabrics that cover the chairs patterned or are they solid color? Are there prints on the wall? What kind of objects are on the shelf? As we begin to assess the details of a room, our first impressions become informed. The more informed we become, the more we are able to make decisions about the kinds of rooms that we want to create for ourselves. By understanding the ingredients that give a room its look and feel we make the kinds of rooms that are right for us.

The mission of this book is to share the recipes that make the right rooms. In doing so we hope to demystify decoration and make it accessible. Using photographs of our favorite rooms, style boards that we have created, and text, *Room Recipes* describes the characteristics that create rooms. Our hope is that it will initiate design novices into the world of decoration and reinforce design ideas for the more experienced. It will address problems and solutions inherent in creating these rooms. Most important, it will offer a blueprint for creating rooms that are visually stimulating and highly personal.

And, like all recipes, all you need to do is adjust slightly, to taste.

graphicstandards

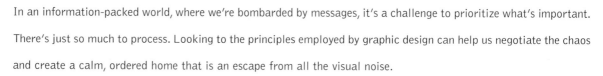

GRAPHIC ROOMS SPEAK OF URBANITY, AND REVEAL UNCOMMON, NONTRADITIONAL OCCUPANTS—YOUNG, ORDERLY, ARTISTIC, AND IRREVERENT PEOPLE.

In an information-packed world, where we're bombarded by messages, it's a challenge to prioritize what's important. There's just so much to process. Looking to the principles employed by graphic design can help us negotiate the chaos and create a calm, ordered home that is an escape from all the visual noise.

The notion of graphic-ness is one of clarity and precision. Graphic design is used to convey identity and to send clear messages. We speak of something being graphic when it is clear and well described (sometimes so vividly that it is uncomfortable, like the "graphic" description of a crime). A graphic designer's world is one in which information is distilled and made aesthetically pleasing. Devices such as editing and cropping are used to focus on what designers want us to see.

Apply the same principles to interior design, and the results are rooms that, at first glance, are clean and to-the-point. Imagine the kind of rooms that a graphic designer might choose to live in. These spaces would have nothing extraneous. They would be visually cool. Graphic design exists in the realm where art meets technology, so these rooms would, likewise, be hip and modern.

Graphic rooms are dedicated to structure, clarity, shape, and order. They have a calm about them, but with an edge. Their calm is in their apparent simplicity, but these rooms also have depth: they are reflections of their inhabitants. They are simple but not passive; they make you think. They use irony as a decorative device, leaving aside any historical references to decoration, save some allusions to the 1950s, 1960s, and 1970s. These rooms are colorful, witty, and slightly irreverent.

Of all the rooms in a home, the kitchen, the hub of the house, needs to function the most smoothly. Order is created in the highly graphic approach to this kitchen. The horizontal quality of the kitchen cabinets (reinforced by floating the cabinets on aluminum legs) parallels a series of windows that run along the back wall. The exposed structure, painted white, adds a graphic element to the kitchen's ceiling. Strong color punctuates the kitchen's neutral palette.

The "standards" part of graphic standards is a way of thinking about materials. The materials used to create these rooms are pretty basic: paint, plastic laminate, solid-colored carpets, common light fixtures, and simple furnishings. But what makes the materials seem so interesting is that they are used like a graphic designer uses type, color, and scale—with precision. They are chosen carefully, with the overall scheme in mind. When risky colors and inventive shapes are key ingredients in a room, what might look loose and whimsical is probably carefully considered. One needs to plan a bit before painting a single wall acid green, or before using eight different plastic laminates or as many drawers in one cabinet.

ABOVE LEFT Blocks of color are key elements in creating graphic interiors. Think of a room as a series of planes, with each plane treated as a whole. In this case, one wall is green, another wall is white, the plane of the table-top is black, and the bent plane of the chairs is white. Even the table base could be considered a single warped plane and it is, likewise, given a single color. The sideboard is color-blocked by using a separate color on each door, the concept further reinforced by each door being a slightly different size—one is even a different material. The color field painting above the sideboard reiterates the color-blocking theme. The tangerine table base is a surprising antidote to the cooler colors.

ABOVE RIGHT A few simple design moves give these cabinets a light-hearted, whimsical character. Rounding the corners of the cubes and the cabinet doors, choosing very mixed colors for the cabinet fronts, and varying height and depth just slightly make the cabinets feel animated. The colors of the doors are set off by the simple white of the cabinets and walls. Small black pulls jump around the cabinet faces, giving them a happy, anthropomorphic quality.

In the graphic layout of a page, the term white space refers to the blank space around an image or text. It makes that element more important by separating it from the visual clutter that surrounds it—a principle that was applied to this room, where the metal bed is allowed space to breathe. The high-gloss painted floor grounds the bed with color, but the reflection allows it to float. Using another graphic design technique, the brilliant blue blanket gets a green border, drawing even more attention than it would have without the border.

OPPOSITE Strong, clear colors and a highly structured composition give this cabinet a playful, abstract quality and a sculptural presence usually reserved for a less functional object. Horizontal and vertical members of the twelve-square composition are strategically missing in order to have a variety of cubby shapes for displaying objects. Alternating warm and cool colored drawers creates strong horizontal lines bound by the extreme vertical shape of orange doors. The hardware gives a secondary compositional structure to the cabinet, and punctuates the horizontal and vertical lines of the cabinet.

ABOVE Though there's nothing better than stealing a few hours in the hush of a home library to read a good book, libraries are usually rather stuffy rooms. The upholstery is often dark, and the woodwork and bookshelves even darker. Not here. The curving bookshelf seems to offer up books that appear to be sliding into our hands, lending a capricious air to this reading room.

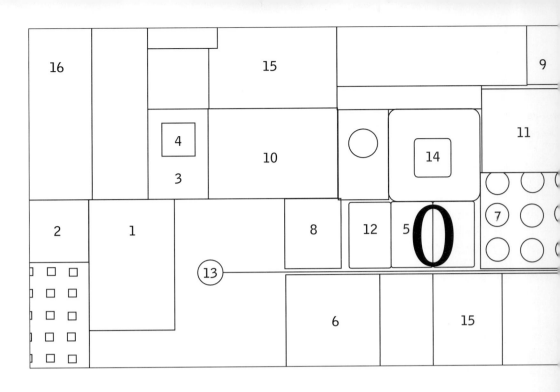

list of ingredients

graphicstandards

1
Perforated metal
Perforated metal is most often used
for commercial suspended ceilings.
Out of that context, in a residential
interior, its color and machined
pattern make it an ideal graphic
material. Use it to front cabinets,
to cover radiators, or to create
a translucent screen.

2
Vinyl tile
The great grandchild of the vener-
able linoleum, these 12" x 12"
(30 cm x 30 cm) vinyl tiles are
one of the least expensive flooring
available. Vinyl tiles come in many

colors, and can easily be used
to create graphic floor patterns,
whether they are bright, over-
scaled checkerboards or subtle
diagonal stripes.

4
Brushed stainless steel hardware
Cabinet and drawer pulls in pure
geometric shapes can give far more
character to a room than their
small size might suggest. In a
kitchen or any room with built-in
cabinets, the repetition paired with
the pure geometry of round or
square pulls conveys a strong sense
of order. A brushed stainless-steel
finish gives the pulls a modern feel.
To underscore the graphic look,
consider using hardware with
a black finish.

3
High gloss surfaces
Cover a wall or cabinet with shiny,
bright color to instantly add
graphic appeal to a simple surface.
Paint the drawer fronts of an old
chest bright yellow and attach
modern pulls. Paint each drawer
a different color, and then add
a glossy layer of lacquer.

5
Aluminum letters
First used to label telephone poles,
aluminum numbers and letters convey a fresh and modern feel to an
interior. Attach them to the front
of drawers or storage bins to offer
a whimsical, graphic approach to
organizing.

oadloom carpet

strong colored broadloom carpet
ill anchor all the other colors in
room. For a more dramatic
ffect, think about using this
tandard floor covering in a new
ay. Instead of using one color
hroughout a room, use two or four
dividing the room in half or in
uadrants. Make an area rug by
ombining four strong colors and
ordering them with a fifth.

**ubber flooring with a raised
ot pattern**

he subtle repetitive pattern
rubber flooring material adds
graphic quality to a kitchen,
athroom, or mudroom. This
ooring is available in bright
imary colors in addition to
ack or gray, as well as square
t and diamond plate patterns.

olored wood flooring

use wood flooring graphically,
range more than one species in a
ttern—alternating mahogany and
aple, or ash and oak. To enhance
e graphic quality of the floor,
int the wood with colored stain,
e effect will infuse a room with
lor, yet retain the warmth of the
tural wood grain.

9
Translucent plastic storage containers

In the 1960s a plastic storage
container was the de riguer home
accessory in every modern interior
and hippie crash pad. Still manufactured in the same factory in
California, these containers are
available in a large variety of
colors and sizes, and lend a very
graphic approach as canisters or
other kinds of storage.

10
Woven vinyl floor covering

Woven vinyl floor covering is a
versatile, sturdy material, long
popular in Europe, but just
becoming readily available in the
United States. It is installed like
sisal or broadloom, and comes in
many colors and patterns. Unlike
these other wall-to-wall materials,
it can be cleaned with a mop.

11
Corrugated plastic

Borrow from commercial materials:
Corrugated plastic or fiberglass
can be brought inside from the
carport roof to sheath a wall or
divide a room.

12
Plastic laminate

To transform the ordinary into the
unique, clad cabinets, counters,
and tabletops in plastic laminate
in exuberant color combinations
and shapes. Readily available and
inexpensive, plastic laminate is
the mainstay for creating graphic
interiors.

13
Simple curtain rod

In more traditional interiors,
curtain rods and, indeed, the
curtains themselves can become
elaborate. This simple rod calls
for plain rings and understated
brackets (even screw eyes) to
create an elegant modern effect.
Used with solid fabric or fabrics
with geometric patterns (stripes
or dots), this window treatment
instantly becomes graphic. This is
a custom item, but it could easily
be made by a metal-smith.

14
Colored glass

Color and shape need to be striking
to stand up to a graphic approach.
Whether it is this dish with rounded
corners, a bud vase, or a bowl to
hold fruit, brightly colored glass
in simple but strong shapes evokes
modernity.

15
Fabrics

Combine blue and green striped
velvet, green textured wool, orange
hopsack, red and yellow hounds-
tooth check, and turquoise stripes
—these fabrics work together
because of their saturated palettes
and matte surfaces. The patterns
are graphic (stripes and checks)
and bold. This is not a place for
delicate fabrics like silk or satin.
Other graphic standard fabrics
that would work well include
vinyl, rubber, or synthetic fabrics
in strong colors.

16
Perforated flannel

Gray flannel is as traditional an
apparel fabric as you can find, at
one time synonymous with poodle
skirts and crafts projects.
Perforated, it has an unusual,
sophisticated, and subtly graphic
effect. Make a Roman blind to
cover a window, allowing a graphic
pattern of light to filter into the
room. Or, back the flannel with
a bright color that complements
other hues in the room and use it to
upholster a chair or make a pillow.

colortheory

IT TAKES A STRONG, INDEPENDENT CHARACTER TO LIVE WITH SATURATED EXUBERANT COLOR.

It's often thought of as a courageous act to paint walls in a bold hue. Hence, when someone doesn't know what color to use, they often choose some version of white. It seems safe. White goes with everything. Or does it? When walls that are not part of an overall white scheme are painted white, everything else in the room leaps into the foreground. You don't notice the room, you notice the things in the room. Suddenly, items with no provenance become conspicuous. Demure dining tables take center stage; mediocre paintings scream for attention. That is why white walls work so well in museums where walls are meant to be a neutral surface, a non-competing backdrop. They act as a light box, spreading light evenly across the room. Entering a room in a museum, you are drawn to the artwork. White makes the art "pop." It isn't always the ideal when it happens in your home.

Strong colors are not always outrageous. In traditional decoration, deep color on walls came from silk and paper that was applied to the wall. Crimson damask parlors or libraries with forest green walls seem masculine and clubby. Most traditional strong colors are dark or light, but not usually bright. Red is one exception, used to refer to Asian sensibilities or classical Pompeian décor. Nineteenth-century Scandinavian rooms are another exception, sometimes painted bright green or deep aqua. A stroll around Beacon Hill in Boston or Rittenhouse Square in Philadelphia—at dusk when views of interiors are the most abundant—demonstrates that peach, salmon, and coral though bright, are perfectly acceptable society colors.

Bright mixed colors seem the most outlandish: chartreuse, magenta, purple, cyan. Process colors. Caribbean colors. Colors reserved for grabbing attention in packaging or athletic apparel. These are the colors that take a certain amount of spirit to endure. It takes a strong, independent character to live with saturated exuberant color and thus, inhabitants of these rooms seem carefree, exotic, somewhat larger than life, perhaps a bit zany, and as colorful as the walls.

Collections are created by assembling like objects. The sum is often greater than the parts. Assembling pieces that are alike, and that also share the same palette, doubles the visual strength of the collection. The strong red-yellow-orange palette of this collection is beautifully outlined against the cooler blue background.

There are two major techniques for decorating with strong color: monochromatic or in a riot of different colors. Although there are always exceptions, two colors have the effect of being monochromatic or, at the very least, well planned. Three strong colors have a joyful, primitive, full-of-life attitude. Using four or more colors is courageous indeed

ABOVE LEFT AND RIGHT If you've been to a party where most of the guests are dressed in tasteful, basic black, there is no denying the power of the guest who enters the room in hot, bright color. At first, there is a moment of surprise, quickly followed by an appreciation for the celebratory nature of color and the daring of the wearer. The same can be said of a room. Surely, there is safety—correctness even—in painting a room off-white or pale gray, but using saturated color is a bold move that allows the rest of the decoration to be active, interesting, and unexpected.

Bold color need not only be reserved for active spaces. Saturated color is an interesting foil for more traditional furnishings. Here, fresh white linens and upholstered headboard are elegant against a hot pink wall, making the room feel like springtime—even in the middle of January.

Paintings are often hung with a lot of space around them on white walls, but here the artist has broken the rules and covered the walls of his room with artwork creating a wallpaper-like effect.

OPPOSITE A stripe running down the center of the hallway exaggerates the length and creates perspective, reiterated by the chair and painting at the end. The chairs running along the sides add a regal touch.

RIGHT An aubergine chair sports red and magenta throw cushions in a lavender bedroom. A grass-green silk sofa is right at home in a chartreuse living room. Monochromatic —a decorating scheme usually reserved for all white or cream-colored rooms—is equally effective with vibrant colors.

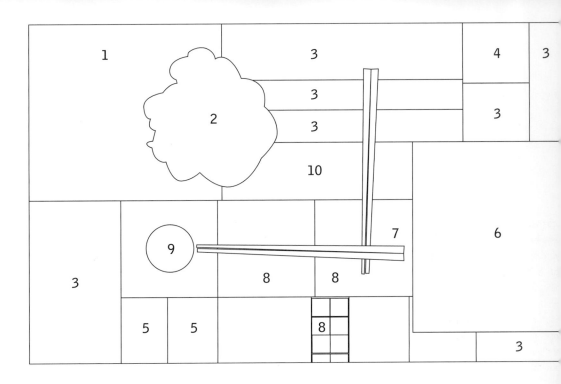

list of ingredients

colortheory

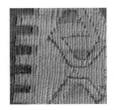

1
Flat weave carpets
Kilim carpets offer an unusual
palette and a more casual feeling
than most other traditional carpets.
The hand-woven carpets have a
very flat weave and a tribal
sensibility.

2
Plastic beads
Beaded curtains, whether
reminiscent of either 1960's crash
pads or North African
caravanserai, create an exotic,
colorful entranceway.

3
Boldly colored fabrics
There are two ways to create rooms
with strong color schemes. Using
fabrics that reiterate the palette of
the wall is the monochromatic
approach. The bolder approach
incorporates two, three, or even four
strong colors together. A word of
caution—certain colors can vibrate
when used together. Mix either all
warm or all cool colors. If you want
to be daring, however, add one chilly
hue into a warm mix.

4
Bullion Fringe
Color can undo tradition. Even
traditional details like bullion fringe
take on a fresh, modern feel in
colors like magenta. Trim
punctuates the lines of upholstered
furniture. Hefty bullion fringe is
used at the base of a sofa or chair
but could also be used at the
bottom of curtains.

.eather and suede

.eather and suede—real or
ynthetic—are extremely durable,
turdy fabrics that are easy to
naintain. Traditionally produced in
rown, tan, or black, these
naterials are now available in a
ost of vibrant colors that look very
nodern and can be used in any
oom of the house.

amask

trongly colored damask fabrics,
vith their symmetrical patterns and
ase-and-plant motifs, are usually
nought of as a formal fabric,
ardly appropriate for a bold room.
ut this is not always the case.
nce the punctuation in an
therwise muted scheme, damask
ow is part of the riot of color.

7
Table settings

When using strong color in a room,
use color even for the accessories.
If a dining room is chrome yellow
or tangerine, choose dinnerware,
flatware, and linens that support
the room. Table settings can change,
so it's a great opportunity for
playful accessories—like these
nontraditional chopsticks.

8
Handmade tiles

Handmade tiles with slightly
irregular edges are a great foil
for strong, processed color. A lime
green stripe of tile in a bathroom
or on a backsplash goes a long
way in adding punch to a room.

9
Decorative knobs and pulls

Good decoration is often in the
details. Doorknobs, drawer pulls,
and handles dramatically change
the look of a piece of furniture.

10
Trim

Smaller bullion fringe or flatter
trims can be used to add a jolt
of color to the edge of pillows
or lampshades.

cottagelife

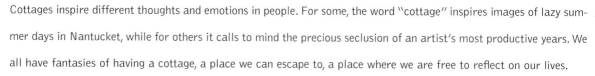

COTTAGES ARE LIKE SCRAPBOOKS— THEY ARE REPOSITORIES OF HAPPY MEMORIES, ACHIEVEMENTS, AND RITES OF PASSAGE.

Cottages inspire different thoughts and emotions in people. For some, the word "cottage" inspires images of lazy summer days in Nantucket, while for others it calls to mind the precious seclusion of an artist's most productive years. We all have fantasies of having a cottage, a place we can escape to, a place where we are free to reflect on our lives.

Cottages and their contents tell a story and this kind of interior is so seductive because everyone has a story to tell. We cherish our history. The cottage is a way of preserving that history, giving it a home, and letting others in to that world. In a cottage, weathered paint, hammer-marked worktables, and hand-worn handrails all become signs of history rather than opportunities for maintenance. Aged surfaces are preserved rather than updated.

Time seems different in a cottage. Hobbies are encouraged and proudly displayed. Useless treasures are kept as reminders of experiences: rocks of a particular color and shape, leaves, things collected from the natural world speak of keen observation and idle time. Collections become testaments to leisure time. You cannot collect beach glass on Wall Street.

Cottages are like scrapbooks—they are repositories of happy memories, achievements, and rites of passage. To the observer of a scrapbook, the contents look like disparate elements. Photos, menus, ticket stubs, phone numbers jotted hastily on scraps of paper. But to the creator, each ticket stub recalls the whole concert, each element conjures an entire experience.

Cottages are class resistant. A very wealthy family may have a cottage, a farm family may have one, but cottages are not about the value of worldly possessions—they are simply about the spirit of possessions. Along the Maine coast, cottages are often rambling Victorian structures that, though enormous, fulfill exactly the same function as a two-room structure with a picket fence: an escape from daily life.

It is not a surprise that this is a popular way to decorate a home. Ironically, it is a difficult look to capture. There are no rules. Quirkiness is natural in a cottage, but there is a fine line between quirkiness and kitsch. Because this style has captured the hearts of many, the home furnishing industry has been happy to reproduce it—with

Pegboard provides a humble, hardworking wall surface for pots and pans. Usually available at the local hardware store, it can be painted any color and outfitted with S hooks to accommodate any arrangement of cooking utensils. Outlining the shape of each object on the pegboard insures that it will go back in just the right spot.

varying results. While cottage style can go overboard, perhaps in the form of mailboxes decorated with colonial blue

ducks adorned with coordinated gingham bows, there are also craftsman who create beautiful reproductions with

doors that are worn where they really would have been worn, and with finishes that look aged.

Creating a cottage space is like planting a garden. You can put the basic structure in place, but it takes a

long time to realize what you set out to accomplish. But if you have the time and the patience to begin these kinds

of rooms and let them mature, what better place to escape from the world than at home.

ABOVE LEFT Cottage-style decorating is "casual." There are no hard and fast rules. Framed photographs share space with unframed ones. Furniture is placed unexpectedly— like this table nestled under the mantelpiece. A found sign is a whimsical piece of art.

ABOVE RIGHT A cottage is often a repository for memories. A summer spent collecting beach glass, an unusually warm weekend in the middle of winter, a week spent with unexpected guests. In this cottage bedroom, the wallpaper has been intentionally peeled away, as if by removing each layer those memories might be revealed.

In a cottage, weathered paint and distressed wood become part of the history and charm of the house. There is beauty in the way wood becomes worn. In another setting, this door might be scraped, sanded, and painted; here, it is just right.

POSITE In cottages, design rules are broken. Scouring local
rd sales and flea markets produces a host of furnishings and
cessories that can be painted, papered, or rebuilt. A porch
ing can take the place of a sofa in the living room and
ces from a word game can decorate a lampshade.

OVE The history of a cottage is revealed in the accumula-
n of objects. Unlike a more formal house, these objects,
llected over time, are not arranged in any particular way,
t layered. There are piles of things everywhere. In this
ttage, the technique of layering is reiterated by the use
different patterned chair fabrics played against the map
the wall.

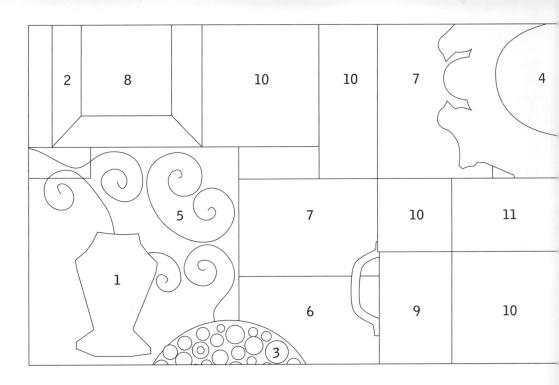

list of ingredients

cottagelife

1
Shard art
Rustic cottage style finds an analogy in shard art. It is romantic, nostalgic, worn, yet beautiful. Sometimes called memory ware, shard art was often produced as a ritual, created from objects from the deceased as a tribute to their life. It has the poignant evidence of a human hand, a very special touch in a fast-paced, hands-off world.

2
Rustic twig picture frame
Objects made from twigs and branches speak volumes about cottage style. Their handmade quality suggests that they were constructed as a hobby and their rustic look fits nicely into interiors filled with patina and weathered-paint surfaces.

3
Button crafts
Buttons are nostalgic. They are both useful and decorative and seem to endure long after the garment they have secured is gone. It is fitting that in the cottage where handcrafted objects are proudly displayed, a spray of button flower or an old button board seems right at home.

4
Mexican tin mirror

The hand-hammered tin mirror from Mexico is warm toned and has a naive quality that is reminiscent of cottage life. The birds suggest the outdoor world and are a natural fit alongside rocks, leaves, and other found objects.

Handwrought metal shelf bracket

Cottages are repositories of happy memories. There's never enough room to display all the things that are the reminders of those memories. Table surfaces become quickly filled. Shelf brackets of hand wrought metal with a rust finish and simple wooden shelves make more room and don't take up the floor space reserved for rocking chairs and napping sofas.

6
Mismatches

Flea markets and yard sales are the perfect spot when it comes to outfitting a cottage. In an urban setting, mismatched dishes, towels, or bed linens might seem like an eyesore, but for the cottage, there's nothing more charming. It is a way to preserve the history of all those that visited before, leaving behind things that would be used happily, again and again.

7
Stripes and checks

Humble fabrics work best in the cottage. Simple checks and plaids or ticking stripes are relaxed and casual, making them especially good candidates for slipcovers. If the fabrics are easy to care for and washable, they're a hands-down winner.

8
Homespun carpets

Carpets with a hand-made feel and a chunky texture embody the cottage spirit—warm, cozy, nostalgic. Hooked, braided, or rag carpets are a natural choice.

9
Aged wood

In the cottage, aged surfaces are preserved rather than updated. Paint that is chipped off or peeling is evidence of a history of experiences.

10
Fabric pieces

Collecting small pieces of fabric, especially those with embroidery or other evidence of handwork, make great pillows or table covers in cottages—all the better if these scraps of fabric have a family provenance.

11
Oilcloth

Oilcloth, a popular 1950's fabric, is available by the yard once again. Great for outdoor use on picnic tables, it also works well indoors. Besides being easy to clean, it's bright colors and whimsical patterns are charming.

sparechairs

Here, there is just enough to NOURISH THE SOUL while ELIMINATING ALL THE CLUTTER

Envision an elegant nineteenth-century Connecticut or Pennsylvania farmhouse, most likely built for a "gentle-man farmer." The house is empty of everything but bare essentials: a bed, a sink, a dining table. Each room is painted a beautiful, soft, light, elegant color. The rooms are infused with light from uncovered or veiled windows. The combination of color and light make the walls luminous. The effect is not minimal, it is simple.

Beginning with surroundings such as this, the spaces need to be adorned with objects that are "just so." It isn't that no item will be extraneous, but each one should be chosen for what it will add to the whole effect of the house. Nothing will be chosen randomly. Even when the house is filled with collections, it will still be spare.

If a single object type could typify this sensibility, it might be a chair. Chairs are interesting objects in their form-function relationship. The function of a chair is simple—to relieve our bodies from the stresses caused by gravity. And yet, unlike a bed, a chair allows us to carry out tasks: we can work while in a chair, we can eat, we can read. We spend most of our waking hours in a chair. Raising a plane 18" off the ground will serve the basic function of a chair as a place to sit—the rest is embellishment.

The sole function of decoration is to create spaces that suit us—both aesthetically and ergonomically. There are infinite ways to achieve these goals, but this style assumes that it can be done with the simplest means. The same might be said for minimal interiors, but in that case, minimalism is the goal, not simplicity. In interiors designed to be minimal, everything is eliminated. Here, there is just enough to nourish the soul while eliminating all the clutter—there is enough to tease the true pack rat, if not nearly enough to satisfy him. The eliminating process is more poignant, less obvious than it is for the true minimalist. This aesthetic allows for collections, albeit edited ones, but collections nonetheless. It also allows for typical spatial elements to be articulated in traditional terms: walls may

Long tables like those found in libraries or camps make great dining tables. The patinaed surface and simple lines more than make up for the fact that they are often narrower than more conventional dining tables. White plates, just-ironed linen napkins, and simple stemware make wonderful accents to these tables.

have baseboards and crown moldings, windows are framed, floors might be worn and allowed to remain that way. The idea of things being iconic and typical is highly valued in this kind of space. Abstraction is not, in any way, a part of this aesthetic the way it is in, say, an all white loft with polished concrete floors. Chipped paint and worn surface are valued for their reference to use and history.

ABOVE LEFT An old piece of furniture can be revitalized with a fresh coat of paint. Milk paint offers a particularly interesting finish. Flat and chalky, it dries quickly and is extremely durable. Milk paint is sold as a powder that is mixed with water and is available in a number of colors.

ABOVE RIGHT Collecting need not be an expensive habit. Everyday objects in beautiful colors and pleasing shapes, like this set of 1940's nesting bowls, can be flea market finds. The trick is in the editing.

Keep the arrangement of objects—flowers, candles, a bowl of apples—low on a dining table to encourage dinner conversation as guests see eye-to-eye. It also is appropriate for this intimate dining room as it contributes to a prevailing sense of calm. The hanging pendant fixture is an appropriate alternative to the expected chandelier.

OPPOSITE A sense of order in a chaotic life is cause for celebration. Though arrangements of objects may be strictly composed it is the addition of warm colors, a textured surface, and a sense of history that keeps rooms restrained but not austere.

ABOVE It is often the organization of things, the way they are arranged, that create special places. Framing a paper sack—albeit one with a Warhol image printed on it—makes the everyday a work of art. Cover bowls of food with a screened dome rather than the ubiquitous plastic wrap to transform a simple meal into a picnic.

LEFT If a single object could typify this design sensibility, it is a chair. Here the chair as a place to sit, as part of an arrangement, and in miniature.

OPPOSITE The old adage that recommends "a place for everything and everything in its place" could be the motto for spare, country style. Shaker baskets arranged in a checkerboard pattern help keep everyday life orderly.

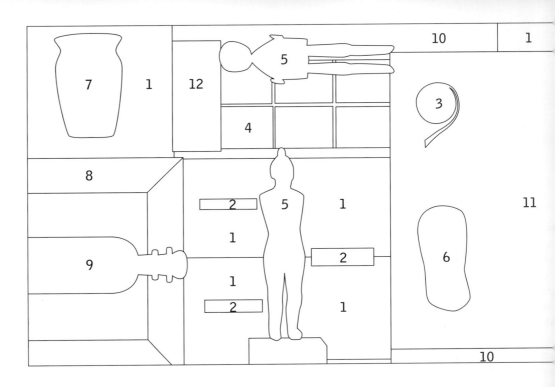

list of ingredients

1

Simple fabrics

Everything in spare, carefully edited interiors has been stripped to their purist form. Fabrics are no exception, made of natural fibers—linen, wool, cotton, silk. There isn't a hint of polyester or plastic. Most often fabrics are used in a natural palette with a delicate play of textures: Smooth billiard cloth counters woven linen and ribbed wool. If pattern is used, it is subtle and cleanly graphic. Tone-on-tone woven linen or monochromatic herringbone silk are two good examples.

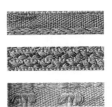

2

Trims

When trim is used, it usually makes a strong statement. It acts as a punctuation mark. Heavy drapery sports long bullion fringe, an over-stuffed pillow is edged with ornate tapes and tassels, a modern sofa is outlined by a brightly colored welt. In spare interiors, if trim is used at all, it is with a light touch. It approximates the color of the fabric it is used with. If the trim has a pattern, it is subtle. A pale gray wool chair might be trimmed with a pale gray, finely textured tape, while a natural linen pillow gets a natural colored cord.

3

Grosgrain ribbon

A thin grosgrain ribbon, a strong, closely woven corded fabric, migh be used to tie a package or used t discreetly edge a lampshade, pillo or a print.

aint palette

he combination of color and light
akes walls luminous. In fact, in
room that gets a lot of natural
ght, very little color is needed.
his palette, using Benjamin Moore
aints, only hints at color, which
all that is needed for rooms
at are reduced save for a few
ell edited pieces of furniture and
jects. Even when choosing colors
is discreet, be sure to paint large
atches on the wall before paint-
g an entire room. Look at the
atch throughout the day to
ake sure it the right color for
particular room.

lk art

ere is a straightforward quality
folk art. It is often made of
mble materials and bears the
amp of the craftsman—highly
lued qualities to people that
abit rooms that speak of sim-
city and beauty. Though highly
rsonal this eighteenth-century
ardian figure from the Philippines
d American wooden doll have
iversal appeal. In spare interiors,
ere is nothing randomly chosen.
jects are carefully selected and
e often part of a highly edited
lection. Everything has a place.

6
Shoe form

This shoe form from Mexico is
covered with milagros—small
charms that petition saints for
help or protection.

7
Pottery

To build a collection, objects need
not be rare or expensive. They need
only to be thoughtfully chosen.
When putting together a collection,
careful attention should be paid
to the objects' specific attributes.
This vase is part of a collection
that includes only vases that are
blue-green, have a simple shape,
and are well priced. A word of
warning: If you want to display
a well-edited, beautiful collection,
practice restraint at flea markets
and yard sales.

8
Linen picture frame

A gilt or carved picture frame just
doesn't seem right in a spare interior. Instead, try using a linen liner
that is normally used to mat a
painting, as the frame itself. It's
simple and elegant and available
at most frame shops.

9
Apothecary jar

The apothecary jar with its ground
glass stopper is just the right kind
of unadorned container for this
spare interior. In the bathroom,
it's great for holding bath salts or
bath oils. In the kitchen, try using
it to bring water to the table—or
better yet, leave it empty and line
more than one on the windowsill
and let sunlight filter through.

10
Woven flat weave carpet

To help create a serene envelope
for spare, chic rooms, use flat
woven carpets in neutral colors
on a wood floor. Though close
to the color of the floor, they
add texture and warmth.

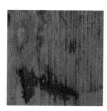

11
Distressed wood

If a room could be described as
repressed, rooms that are strictly
ordered and highly edited might fit
that description. Using materials
that show wear—a worn spot on
the handle of a rocking chair for
instance—helps to erase that label.

12
Sheer linen

Sheer linen check fabric in close
colors is great for window coverings. Light coming through the
fabric further erases the already
subtle color difference.

woodworks

DARK, CARVED WOOD IS BARONIAL AND TRADITIONAL.
PANELED ROOMS WITH KNOTTY PINE ARE RUSTIC.
SMOOTH, FLUSH WOOD CABINETS ARE MODERN.

After a lecture in the 1970s, Richard Meier, an architect well known for producing stark white buildings, was asked to comment about why he painted wood white. "It doesn't seem natural," commented the questioner. Meier explained that once you're beyond the log, as in a log cabin, wood used in the service of architecture is hardly natural. It is planed, sawn, tortured into molding by being shaped with knives, varnished, oiled, rubbed, and sprayed. There is nothing left about it that is natural.

Regardless of whether it is natural or not, when wood predominates interiors, the spaces are said to have a warmth about them. What is it about wood that predisposes us to use the word "warm" in relation to it? Is it partly that it really is warm unlike stone or metal or plastic? But it's not really tactile warmth that we speak about, it's visual warmth. Unless treated with aniline dyes in a cool color range, the natural coloration of wood is warm.

Wood is a material with enough character that, its virtues are still apparent even when it is painted. Painted wood still shows grain and texture, it still has a certain softness. The character of wood is strong enough that even wood products like cork, plywood, paper, and fiberboard, still have a lot of the attributes of wood. However processed they are, however far they are from being a tree trunk, they still feel down to earth.

Wood delivers several strong messages when used as a major ingredient of a room. The effect can be manipulated depending on how it is used. Dark, carved wood is baronial and traditional. Paneled rooms with knotty pine are rustic. Smooth, flush wood cabinets are modern. At the end of the 1990s, it seemed that every store at the mall was a combination of maple or fir and stainless steel or brushed aluminum—a combination meant to be forward thinking. Though wood is currently a cozy antidote to the electronic world, it has been, in recent history, a product symbolizing significant technological advance. Thonet's bent wood rocker and Eames' potato chip chair both speak of change.

A collection of mismatched chairs often creates a more interesting room. The chairs should have a similar sensibility, like this collection of Thonet bent wood chairs. Make sure chair heights are the same, ensuring that dinner guests see eye-to-eye.

Currently, key ingredients from the wood family are English oak, Wenge, and ebony. Dark polished surface are the perfect counterpoint to hand-wrought wood artifacts like African stools and masks. Recently, wood floor have been darker and set off by white walls. But whether Meier's painted white wood of the 1970s or the dark woo of today, wood has always been a key ingredient in contemporary interiors.

ABOVE LEFT A modern bench, inspired by African stools, does double duty. Not only does it provide a place to sit, but acts as a surface on which to display art. Art doesn't always need to be hung on the wall to be appreciated, it can often sit on the floor or a mantle and lean against a wall.

ABOVE RIGHT Dining tables are often surrounded with chairs that are either fully upholstered or upholstered on the seats. Common wisdom tells us that these types of chairs not only provide more comfortable seating (allowing diners to linger at the table long after the meal is over), but add warmth to the room. As this set of T. H. Robsjohn-Gibbings chairs demonstrates, this is not always the case.

Small stools serve as both side tables and extra seating. African stools, often carved from a single piece of wood, are widely varied ranging from simple three-legged styles to elaborately carved pieces.

BELOW Ceilings are often taken for granted, usually painted white and never thought about again. Here a plywood ceiling not only adds interest to the room, it creates another plane while adding warmth to the modern space.

OPPOSITE A modern stairway that could feel stark or even foreboding if freestanding is made friendlier by the introduction of varying types of wood. A row of floor-to-ceiling wooden doors creates a wood wall. Wood floors are left bare. A rough-hewn wood sculpture adds an interesting contrast to the stairway.

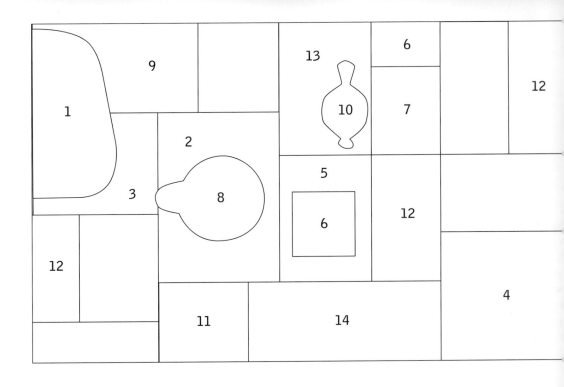

list of ingredients

woodworks

1
Modern plywood chairs
The Eames bent plywood chairs, whose raw materials reflect a response to post-WWII shortage of wood, and were manufactured by Herman Miller, are perhaps the twentieth-century's icon of modernity. Designed mid-century and revived at the end, the marriage of technology with the warmth of wood is irresistible.

2
Paper flooring
Paper floor mats are as visually elegant as sisal mats but much kinder to bare feet. The paper is twisted (like the carry handles of a brown paper bag) and woven in small-scale geometric patterns. It is available in a number of patterns and colors. The overall effect is like Japanese tatami mats. The manufacturer, Merida, recommends sealing the floor covering to allow a little more time to pick up spills.

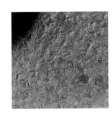

3
Cork
Cork is made from tree bark. Traditionally it was used in institutional settings like libraries and hospitals, but it has a grand residential provenance as well— the walls and floors of the bathrooms at Frank Lloyd Wright's Fallingwater are cork. Cork flooring lends the same kind of visual warmth to a room that wood floors do, but it is resilient and as easy to install as any tile floor.

4
Particle board
Part of a whole family of products made from wood chips with names like medium density fiberboard and flake board, particle board was originally intended for use as a sheathing or as a substrate covered with a "better" material. However, a whole generation of designers has discovered that these materials are perfectly suitable as is and lend an air of "found material" to a room.

Woven raffia

A close relative to grass cloth—the material widely used as wall covering in high style 1960s interiors—raffia is now sold by Donghia as upholstery fabric. Its definitive texture adds a natural elegance to a room.

Bamboo shades

Sometimes used as a shade under fabric curtains and sometimes as the only window covering, bamboo has a very breezy, natural feel. It calls to mind exotic places and filters light in a way that lends a room a feel tropical.

Handmade paper

The infinite variety of handmade papers available (a good craftsman can make their own) can be used to make lampshades or applied to the wall in a grid. It also becomes an important ingredient in a room when used to cover an album of treasured photographs on permanent display.

8
African neck-rest

In a room created predominantly of wood, an African neck-rest, with it's surprisingly modern shape and brilliant dark sheen, adds a sense of tradition and craftsmanship.

9
Kuba cloth

The geometric patterns and warm colors of African textiles are perfect accompaniments for wood.

10
Worn wood

Often, the more wood shows age, use, and wear, the more valuable it becomes as part of a room's design. As the edges of a block of wood soften, so does the character. French farmhouse tables, old wood handrails, antique linen presses— these are the objects that lend a sense of continuity to a space.

11
Stamped leather

Leather can be manipulated into colors and textures that make it almost unrecognizable. It can be woven, distressed, embossed, or perforated. In its more traditional colors, a range of browns from tan to chocolate, leather works well with wood. As an upholstery material leather not only wears well, but it improves with age.

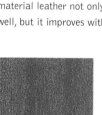

12
Wood veneer

Veneer is a thin sheet of wood that is adhered to a substrate. An incredibly versatile material, wood veneer is used in furniture, cabinetry, and wall paneling. Cutting wood into veneer can create beautiful patterns that are not as readily available in solid wood planks.

13
Parquet flooring

Available in a wide price range —from gymnasium floors to intricately patterned stairhalls— Parquet can be used in both modern and traditional interiors.

14
Printed fabric

Generally designed to be precise, fabrics that are printed with warm colors and uneven, hand-drawn patterns bring a casual ease to a room.

cartwheels

THINGS CREATED PRIOR TO THE CYBER-ERA MAKE US YEARN FOR THE GOOD OLD DAYS.

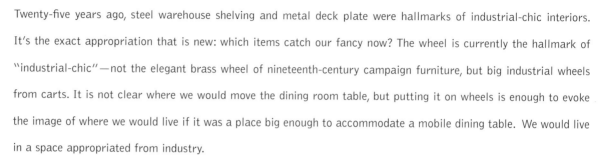

Twenty-five years ago, steel warehouse shelving and metal deck plate were hallmarks of industrial-chic interiors. It's the exact appropriation that is new: which items catch our fancy now? The wheel is currently the hallmark of "industrial-chic"—not the elegant brass wheel of nineteenth-century campaign furniture, but big industrial wheels from carts. It is not clear where we would move the dining room table, but putting it on wheels is enough to evoke the image of where we would live if it was a place big enough to accommodate a mobile dining table. We would live in a space appropriated from industry.

A perusal of the industrial-chic bible *High Tech* by Joan Kron and Susanne Slesin is telling. Written in 1978, the pictures are a bit dated (hairstyles are always a dead giveaway) but the sensibility is surprisingly fresh. A timeless concept, there is very little in the book that wouldn't still look good. The difference is that 25 years ago, the things the authors were suggesting looked cutting edge—now, they look cozy. As technological development speeds up, the gap between cutting-edge and nostalgic has narrowed. Think of the computer you used just ten years ago. Think of your answering machine—or even the telephone you used. It all seems quaint now.

Plastics are so ubiquitous that metal, the mainstay of the look Kron and Slesin proposed, looks natural, honest, and homey. According to *High Tech*, metal plate, embossed to be slip-resistant, was "a common industrial material often used on the floors of battleship boiler rooms." Today, embossed metal plates recall the stoops of early twentieth-century industrial buildings in the Soho section of New York City. We no longer have a current reference, only a historical one. Battleship boiler rooms are no longer part of our communal memory the way raised flooring in a computer room may be.

As a decorating term, industrial-chic can be ambiguous. To some, the word "industrial" implies a hard, cold, impersonal world, while to others, a quirky personal vision. For true devotees of this look, it is the ambiguity that is attractive. Creating an environment with things that were once modern is not about modernity, it is about nostalgia. Objects that were once part of the industrial world now seem naive. Things created prior to the cyber-era make us yearn for the good old days. Electric objects might have exposed conduits to express the path of electricity, to demystify how a thing worked, as if to say, "this isn't magic, it's hard wired."

In this kitchen what is old (when was the last time you saw a rotary telephone) was once thought of as techno—logically advanced. Conversely, like the schoolroom-inspired clock, what is new is often modeled after an old design.

Many of the things in these rooms refer to a time when work was "hands on." The furniture and object might have come from hospitals, laundries, factories, offices (imagine what an insurance office looked like before you ordered insurance online), construction sites, cafeterias, and restaurant kitchens. All of these venues evoke images of good honest hard-working people, images of people that were upstanding members of the community. The kind of work that went on in these kinds of places took teamwork to accomplish. We think of assembly lines as isolated dehumanizing places but in this world, in the world of industrial-chic, there is nothing more chic than a conveyor belt.

ABOVE LEFT AND RIGHT Galvanized trash barrels seem right at home when set against a house sheathed in metal. Prowling the aisles of hardware stores is often the best way to find the right materials to support an industrial aesthetic. This was precisely the way the owners of this house created the chicken wire and conduit trellis that brackets the entranceway.

A home office is created from standard-issue pieces like the stool, filing cabinets, and safety lamp. Part of the main living space, the office is slightly elevated, reminiscent of the "boss's" office, which overlooked the factory.

OPPOSITE The workplace is often thought of as an impersonal environment but a floor of an old factory takes on a much warmer personality when it is converted to living quarters. Though the space is completely open, the placement of furniture implies the function of each area.

ABOVE A colorful collection of industrial-sized spools of thread create a skyline atop a file cabinet. Stacking chairs are usually reserved for commercial settings, but they can be extremely useful at home as well.

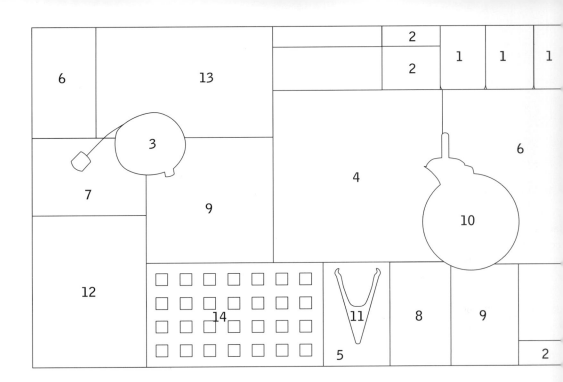

list of ingredients

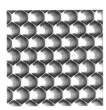

1

Stainless steel

When you think of stainless steel, you usually think of clinical environments, but texture adds a whole new dimension. One of the difficulties of using stainless steel in a residential application, is that it readily shows fingerprints. For a whole new twist, use stainless steel with a woven or even a wood-grain pattern.

2

Gray cowhide and silver leather

Borrowing from the world of fashion, even cowhide looks industrial when it has been given a gray coloring. So does leather when it's been dyed silver. This is as far as you can get from the standard black-and-white pattern of a Holstein that you see roaming on picturesque farms. With almost nothing natural left about them, these materials might be used for the slip seat of a chair or for pillows in an industrial setting. As with many strong ingredients, a little goes a long way.

3

Cable display system

Used by visual display teams and exhibition designers, these systems are an extremely versatile ingredient for creating truly elegant industrial rooms. They are mounted taut, floor-to-ceiling (some systems have wall mounting brackets), and are available with a lot of different types of fittings, some designed to hold glass shelves, others that hold wood shelves and even clips that hold vertical planes of material which can, in turn, be used to display art.

7
Rubber floor mat
Produced for entry vestibules, shower stalls, and locker room floors, rubber mats can be picked up for easy maintenance in areas of the house that tend to get wet or dirty.

10
Wheels
Big industrial wheels are the ingredient that give this look the clearest identity. Wheels are about mobility and flexibility, poignant traits of modern life. Use them for the table that holds the TV for easy viewing —or use them on your bed for easy cleaning.

13
Woven metal
Typically used in a residential setting only as screens to keep insects out, woven metal mesh might also be used in cabinet doors, creating modern pie-safes.

arpet tiles
hese tiles are put to the test in ational retail chains, but out of ontext—in a residential setting— . looks as chic as it is tough. lternating the direction of the rain of the tile creates a subtle heckerboard.

lass tiles
roduced to finish freestanding dges of glass-block walls, the ubtle green color and smooth ounded texture of these glass les creates beautiful surfaces.

8
Cocoa mat
A large expanse of cocoa mat in the entry hall will help keep dirt from the outside world from being brought indoors. It is traditionally used in a natural brown color, but black makes it look less natural and more industrial.

11
Metal clamps
An everyday tool for photographers, clamps can be used at home to attach curtains to a rod fashioned from galvanized pipe, or to secure oilcloth onto a table to protect it from kids' art projects.

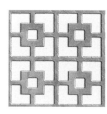

14
Stamped metal
This pattern of stamped metal is most recognizable because it was used as radiator covers. It was usually painted, but left in its natural state, it might make an elegant folding screen. Some stamped metal is a heavy enough gauge to use for shelving.

aw silk
hough not an industrial material, e chunky texture and dark beige olor are a warm, luxurious ounterpoint to cool materials ke metal.

9
Flannel
The mat surface of wool flannel makes it look incredibly modern. Although it is available in a huge array of saturated colors, heathered charcoal and medium gray look appropriately understated for the monochromatic surroundings of rooms like these.

12
Newspaper wallpaper
Like graffiti, wallpaper produced from newsprint can give a room a space a graphic, edgy, urban quality. Using color laser technology, you can produce your own wallpaper with exactly the message you want to send to visitors.

fullhouse

THE PEOPLE WHO CREATE THESE ROOMS ARE NOT AFTER A LOOK, THEY ARE AFTER CHARACTER.

Some people love to be surrounded by things. There is a certain comfort in the fact that wherever their gaze may land, there is the reminder of an experience or the image of a cherished friend. Houses that are filled with things represent an inner life. These rooms represent rich lives, treasure troves of experience. If you found yourself in one of these rooms without knowing the inhabitant, you could reconstruct their world. You could imagine that their ancestors—well documented in framed photos—are your ancestors. You could browse their book collection and understand something profound about them, about their dreams and desires.

These rooms have the quality of a cocoon or a womb. They are places to happily unplug the phone, kick off your shoes, and hole up in. Often they have the quality of night, the quality of a dream. At night, the interior world has no competition from outside views. To the person who lives in a house full of objects, a spare environment—rooms that depend on the light of day to illuminate their best quality—may seem cold, distant, inhuman.

Full rooms break all the rules of decorating. Nothing matches. There is way too much of everything: too many pictures, too many books, too many objects. But for the inhabitants, each and every object is a memory. Eclecticism best describes the decorating sensibility that creates rooms like these. Quoting any one style or period would seem confining and frivolous. The people who create these rooms are not after a look, they are after character. The spaces are extremely personal. The creation of shrines best describes the decorating technique employed to carry out the sensibility. Shrines may take many forms. The most common are walls of family photos, or tablescapes of travel mementos. Rather than finding things that fulfill a predetermined decorative scheme, these rooms are the result of lifelong collections.

Vary materials to add interest and depth to a room. On this sideboard, the surface interest of each of the materials combines to create a vignette that is rich, textured, and strong. Carved wood, hand-forged iron, etched glass and ceramic work well together because of the scale and weight of each piece.

Collecting is more than an activity. It is a general take on the world. To the collector, the collection represents the thrill of the hunt. What is a haven for this type of personality looks to the uninitiated like chaos. Isabella Stewart Gardner in her Boston house and Sir John Soane in his early-nineteenth-century London house are perfect examples of interiors created by collecting on the highest order. But it is not necessarily the worth of the collection that makes these interiors intriguing, it's that they are filled with so much stuff. These interiors are visually delightful. The collections may be whimsical or historical or personal but they always speak of passion of the collector. The hallmarks of this kind of decoration are cross-cultural rooms, densely layered and often exotic.

OPPOSITE To create interest in a room composed of many patterned fabrics, vary the visual strength of each pattern. In this living room, a cut velvet checkerboard fabric is the strongest pattern in the room and calls attention to the library armchair, which has an important pedigree. If every fabric were equally strong, the room would feel "noisy" and unedited.

OPPOSITE Twin framed mirrors create virtual doorways while emphasizing the various patterns at play in this small bedroom. The gardenesque quality of the hand-blocked wallpaper is reiterated on the base of the wooden altar table and by inlaid boxes stacked on the floor.

TOP RIGHT This perfect city apartment—a gracious living room, a dining room that doubles as a study, a cozy bedroom, a dressing area and a storage room—occupies a 16 x 20 space. The proportion, scale and spatial arrangement are the tools used to create a haven for its occupant.

MIDDLE RIGHT To create the bedroom area, dividers were covered with cloth from India on which a framed collection of postcards were hung. This layering of materials enhances the intimate feeling of the space and allows it to be independent from the rest of the room.

BOTTOM RIGHT Mixing patterns can be tricky. Choosing a consistent palette and varying the size of the patterns helps ensure success. The tones of the dressing area are rich and warm and the Indian fabric, with its large bordered inset, complements the small leopard-print wall covering.

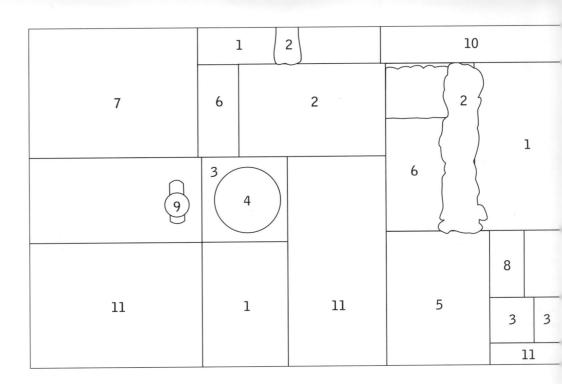

list of ingredients

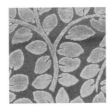

1
Textured cut velvet
Textured fabrics like cut or voided velvet echo the sensibility found in rooms that are filled with objects and furnishings. The richness of texture (created by fabrics of varying pile heights) adds another tier of opulence to the already layered interior.

2
Beads
Beading, whether on fabric or used as trim, represents the rich life embodied in rooms that are densely layered. It is more comparable to the ornate jewelry worn by eighteenth-century royalty rather than the twenty-first century rock star. Bead shops, usually thought of as a resource for jewelry making, are a good resource for finding unusual beads that can be used in interiors as well.

3
Metallic tile
Metallic tiles are available in many finishes—burnished gold, silver, and copper—and in a variety of sizes. The lighting is enriched in rooms that have metallic finishes.

bjects

painted wooden box, the kind
at you might find in a Bombay
urist shop, is an example of the
nsity of pattern and the richness
color that embodies the volup-
ous nature of this kind of interior.

ux finishes

ood surfaces that are elaborately
inted, like this faux tortoiseshell,
e good finishes for small pieces
furniture. Other painting tech-
ques could include faux bois or
ux bamboo.

etallic finishes

allpapers with subtle matte
etallic finishes are a good
ternative to painting. For an
teresting effect, cut the paper
to squares and lay these in a
ock pattern.

7
Carpets

Choose carpets that are richly
colored and highly patterned. When
small carpets are layered on the
floor, a room takes on an exotic feel,
with romantic allusions to faraway
places. Hand woven carpets, rather
than machine-made, imbue the room
with the spirit of the craftsman.

8
Mosaic glass tiles

A bathroom tiled in copper, onyx,
and ruby colored mosaic glass tiles
becomes a jewel box. These tiles can
be used in all one color, randomly
mixed, or in an homebred pattern,
light to dark, down the wall.

9
Decorative cabinet hardware

The hand-hammered recycled brass
knob from Ghana, though quite
small, is nevertheless heavily
detailed. Intricately patterned
hardware or hardware with rich
finishes like English pewter or
antique brass are appropriate
choices for cabinets and drawers.

10
Iridescent silk

There is an almost magical quality
to iridescent silk. The subtle color
shift that occurs when the fabric
rustles or is seen in different light
makes it a particularly appropriate
choice for window coverings.

11
Woven fabrics

In general, woven fabrics, rather
than printed ones should be used
in richly layered interiors as they
help convey the luxuriousness and
authenticity of tradition.

whitewhite

THERE'S IS NO SHADOW TO HIDE IN, NO CLUTTER TO BLEND INTO. WHITE ROOMS DEMAND ABSOLUTE DISCIPLINE.

Maybe it's human nature to imagine our thoughts would be clear and elegant if only our surroundings were. The exclusive use of white in an interior implies control, order, and clarity. If white seems somewhat clinical, it also chic. White rooms are cool, stylish, urbane. Ordinarily, things aren't white and if they are, they get dirty. White yellows with age. Keeping things white suggests that things are fresh, clean, attended to.

White rooms are intriguing. They immediately make you wonder where the inhabitant's real life is hidden. Who could live here? Where's the newspaper? Where are the plastic toys? Where are the stains and nicks and scratches? In an all-white room, dust bunnies seem like dust dinosaurs. White makes order out of chaos by the fact that everything unsightly must be hidden because everything is so visible. There's is no shadow to hide in, no clutter to blend into. White rooms demand absolute discipline.

In a white room, sunlight becomes an important ingredient. It changes the perception of the space. Reflections of surroundings become critical. A blue sky makes the room appear cool. Clouds make the room pale gray, trees make the room green, and the sun reflecting off a brick building across the street makes it appear pink. White rooms bounce light so less is needed to make the room seem bright.

Any source of light changes the perception of white space. Incandescent light makes a white room warm, while fluorescent lends a commercial feel. Candlelight can make the space seem magical. Lighting drastically effects any room, of course, but it is so much more obvious in a white room.

Off-white rooms are more forgiving. The possible range of things that can be included in the recipe for such rooms is much larger. White-white rooms are more absolute. They are more pure and more complex than one generally imagines. There are many shades of white. Texture can make the same white look different. A high-gloss and matte version of the same white will have different effects. A brick wall that has been painted white can seem humble and unassuming, white marble can seem slick.

More than most recipes for rooms, all-white interiors are particularly tricky. They conjure up the image of the designer, unfettered by everyday things, manipulating the meaning of interiors and objects in grand and simple ways.

Spas are often all white. Whiteness offers a respite from the noise of everyday life. All-white rooms have a similar calming effect. Yards of sheer white fabric create soft folds and diffused light, mitigating the starkness of this room and enhancing its soothing qualities.

The same techniques that many fashion photographers use in their studios have been employed in this interior. Gleaming white floors, white walls, and huge windows allow lots of natural light to fill the room even on overcast days.

OPPOSITE A mantelpiece seems unnecessary on this elegant fireplace. The strong black rectangle that is the fireplace is exaggerated by the white marble surrounding. When lit, the fire creates a warm counterpoint to the cool cantilevered shelf.

ABOVE When there are no curves, patinas, or textures to cover up a tricky corner, a troublesome door, or a prickly roof line, exacting details become crucial. Everything is revealed. Spare, modern spaces demand the same level of craftsmanship used to restore historic houses.

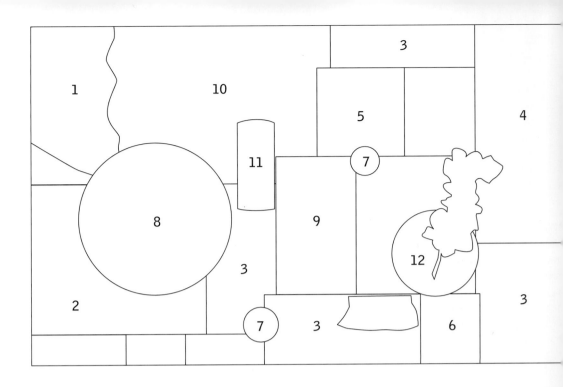

list of ingredients

whitewhite

1
Marble
When an all-white interior demands a hard surface, this veinless marble is the perfect choice. It implies absolute freshness and hygiene, essential traits of all white rooms.

2
Glass
Clear glass for tabletops, shelving, and accessories lends to the purity of white rooms. Glass is an elemental material that speaks to the lucidity of an all-white environment.

3
Textured fabrics
In most design schemes, rooms are informed by the use of a number of coordinated fabrics—one fabric picking up a thread of color from another, which then leads to another and then another. In all-white rooms, it is the varying textures that are created by subtle white-on-white patterns and weaves that create the scheme. The effect of light playing off the quilted pattern of matelasse, the chevron stripe of a herringbone fabric, the ribs of an ottoman cloth, and the open weave of a loosely woven linen create rooms that are cool and stylish.

4
Frosting
Using translucent materials is a wonderful way to diffuse light in a space. Frosted glass has a beautiful green cast. But for the true purist, using frosted plexiglass is a good alternative because it is pristinely white. Hand sanding clear plexiglass not only gives a translucent finish but also an elegant variegated texture.

All-white tile

When choosing ceramic tiles avoid gray-blue or red-brown whites as these will make even the most spotless kitchens and bathrooms appear blemished. White grout, though difficult to maintain, keeps the surface unified.

8
Simple plastic bowl

The frosted plastic bowl does double duty. In the kitchen or dining room it holds ice cream (preferably vanilla) or soup (preferably vichyssoise). In the living room, a line of white bowls may hold pure white stones.

10
Sheer white

Novel fabrics, like this sheer cloth with its algae-like decoration, add an unexpected touch of whimsy to a room that is controlled and ordered.

Solid surfacing

Best known by trade names like Corian, solid surface materials are available in many shades of white. Solid surfacing is as versatile as plastic laminate, but far more luxurious. It can be used on countertops, walls, or tub decks.

9
White paint

There are a host of white paints. In fact, every paint company offers a wide variety. Coupled with the fact that white walls pick up the reflection of the outdoor surroundings, which white paint to use becomes the hardest decision to make in creating an all-white interior. Paint huge swatches in various places throughout the home and watch them during different phases of the day and night before making a final decision. The right white will become evident after careful observation.

11
White silk cord

White silk cord can be used to trim the edge of a pillow or the bottom of a lampshade, encircle a dinner napkin, or tie up a sagging bunch of paper whites.

12
Glass vase

A simple glass vase holding a perfect white flower has become an icon for all white interiors.

White-on-white hardware

To maintain the pristine quality of all-white rooms, keep surfaces unfettered by using white hardware. Look for white ceramic or frosted drawer pulls and handles. Paint door hinges the same color white as the attendant wall or cabinet. It's not hard to find white switch plate covers. And, if hardware can't be pure white, use matte silver metals like stainless steel or brushed nickel.

eleganteclecticism

THESE ROOMS ARE **PERSONAL.** THEY ARE THE RESULT OF A **UNIQUE** SET OF **EXPERIENCES** AND **KNOWLEDGE** AND THE RESULT OF **CAREFUL** EDITING AND **THOUGHTFUL** CHOICES.

It is refreshing to come across someone who knows about a lot of things, who's been to many places, and who can wear their knowledge well. The word dilettante (from the Italian word *dilettare*, meaning "to delight") was used to describe the daily activities of some upper class English gentlemen. A dilettante dabbled in many subjects—from Renaissance painting to classical sculpture to French poetry. He was a generalist. He had roving sensibilities and followed a subject simply for the sake of acquiring the knowledge.

It takes the sensibility of a dilettante to create elegant eclectic rooms. Eclectic rooms do not have an immediate impact, like an all-white room or a rustic cottage might have. It takes some time to absorb the intention of the mix. These rooms are personal. They are the result of a unique set of experiences and knowledge and the result of careful editing and thoughtful choices. There are no rules—only the sensibility and confidence of the designer. And unlike simpler looks that can be put together quickly, eclectic rooms need time to evolve.

Unfortunately, we live in a world of specialists rather than dilettantes. Children specialize in a sport, sometimes at a very young age. Physicians specialize in only one aspect of care. Often even grade school teachers only know how to teach one subject. Generalists are suspect. It is assumed that their knowledge is superficial. The same is true of the decorative schemes of rooms. Things are supposed to go together. Furniture is sold in suites. Rooms should be country or traditional or modern—but not all three at once.

Though the word eclectic is often used to describe a room's decorative scheme, it is a tricky term. In the worst sense, it might be used to describe a room where nothing quite matches or in which an old cabinet from grandmother is incorporated into an otherwise consistent interior. It might encompass the whole house and mean that the library is decorated using carved mahogany and burgundy leather with nail head trim, while the living room has awning stripes, sisal flooring, and white canvas furniture.

Common wisdom suggests that certain fabrics belong on certain types of furniture. Traditional, formal chairs and sofas are usually covered in mohair, velvet, or damask. Not many living rooms sport turn-of-the-twentieth-century furnishings in mattress ticking stripes, but the owners of this Westport, Connecticut home have a keen eye and a roving sensibility that allows for this unusual but effective combination.

But truly eclectic rooms are about the aesthetic relationship of the pieces in the room. Like paginating a magazine or installing an art exhibition, the immediate context is extremely important. A mid-century modern chair may be pulled up to a Directoire desk and the effect can be perfect—or truly awful. Whether or not it works is highly subjective. It may be that the proportion or the texture are just right or that the carpet pulls them together. The pair of objects may refer to a scene in a favorite movie. They may be delightfully tongue-in-cheek. Success in this kind of decorating is hard to define. Usually it takes a good eye and enough self assurance to know that if you are drawn to two seemingly disparate objects, the simple fact that you are drawn to both of them makes them work together.

ABOVE LEFT It takes a trained eye to hang framed neo-classical prints above beds dressed in seersucker stripes and camp plaids like those that might be found at an Adirondack lodge—and make them work together.

ABOVE RIGHT It may take daring to put together rooms that have no clear decorating rules, but it certainly is liberating. Glazed Pompeian red walls, usually reserved for more formal spaces like dining and living rooms, enclose a small guest bedroom. The French Empire bed is casually dressed in layered plaids. The night stand is an old bench picked up at a yard sale.

The true eclectic always mixes things up. In a modern white room with a floating white bench, stripes meet plaids and plaids meet paisley to create a sitting area that feels like an island retreat.

BELOW In the living room, modern art and a formal antique hand-painted screen share wall space. Add a painted country bench brought in from the garden, a Victorian chair covered in mattress ticking, and an antique rusted iron table to the mix, paint the floor very dark green and forget about carpets, and a true eclectic spirit becomes clear.

OPPOSITE The "great wall of china," jokingly referred to by the owners of this house, grew out of their love of travel. Every plate is a memento of a trip they have taken. And though no two plates are alike—or even match—they look great together. A general sensibility, one of careful editing, pervades the entire collection. Emeco aluminum chairs, originally designed for the Navy, sit comfortably around a rustic country table.

Le P. Erigone.

Fig. 4.

Le P. Amathée.

Fig. 4 bis.

Fig. 5.

Fig. 5 bis.

Le P. Octavie.

HISTOIRE NATURELLE, Insectes.

Benard Direxit.

Architecture.

ur la Ligne A.B

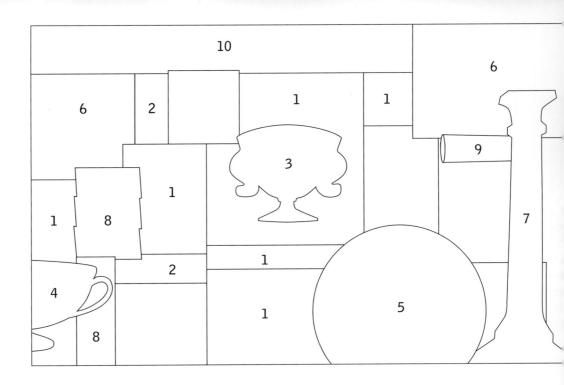

list of ingredients

eleganteclecticism

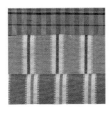

1

Stripes and checks

When it comes to selecting fabric for an eclectic space, try checks and plaids—the mainstay of traditional country cottons—in silk and mix them with humble ticking stripes and boldly colored billiard cloth for just the right effect. When mixing checks and plaids, try pulling out one of the more unexpected colors of the plaid and use it as the lead color for the stripe fabric. Vary the size of the patterns. Pair graphic checks with more complicated plaids or stripes. Trust your instincts.

2

Bold colors

That inhabitants of eclectic rooms are usually interested in many things is evident in many ways. Rooms are put together with bits and pieces of information borrowed from travels, a favorite movie, a cherished book, a piece of art. So it comes as no surprise to find that the palette of these rooms is often bold. Colors like Pompeian red, Tuscan yellow, and Robert Adam blue refer to experiences and memories.

3

Green glass urn

There is a classical element to many of the objects found in eclectic rooms. A small green glass urn with fish-shaped handles is a prized flea market find. Mixed in with a pile of plates from the 1950s and jelly jar juice glasses, it stood out as the perfect accessory for an eclectic space.

Black Wedgewood urn

The elegant, unusual shape—flat and wide—of the black Wedgewood urn makes it the perfect container for letters waiting to be posted. Place it on a hall table next to a lamp as part of an eclectic tableaux.

Neoclassical plate

This hand-painted plate, part of a set of ten that each have a different classically inspired design, was found at an antique shop. Though the plates have no important provenance, they could look great hanging on either side of a doorway or in a pyramid shape on the wall. When hanging an arrangement of plates—or multiple prints—line up the configuration on the floor first. This avoids unnecessary holes in the wall.

6
Antique prints

Depending on your budget, there are many good resources for antique as well as reproduction prints. Choose classical architecture, garden plans, and botanical studies as the subject and border with a simple black or a gilt frame. If framing isn't in the budget try clip frames—two pieces of glass that sandwich the print. Hang prints symmetrically above a chair or over a table for just the right look.

7
Candlestick lamp base

Even if lighting is modern it can still be classically informed. Choose classically shaped lamp with a column, urn, or candlestick base. This lamp base had an oak finish that was painted dark green to complement the rich palette.

8
Wooden Venetian blinds

Wooden blinds are a good alternative to curtains. They come in a number of wood finishes and depending on the size of the window and the look that you're after, slats are available in 1- and 2-inch widths (though some companies offer custom sizing). Cord or tape is available in a host of colors to finish the look of the blinds. Two-inch slats in a walnut finish is a typical choice for an elegant interior.

9
Curtain rod finial

There is so much information in an eclectic room mix that it is often a good idea to keep hardware simple. (Unless of course, there's a Murano glass doorknob brought back from a trip to Venice or an antique drawer pull from the Paris flea market.) This simple metal curtain rod finial has just enough detail to keep it interesting yet not over power any of the objects in the room.

10
Wool carpet runner

The elegant flat weave of this carpet makes it a great option for stairs. Though stripes can only be used on straight runs—curved stairs or windows will make the stripes chaotic—they are a classic alternative to solids or florals.

flowerpower

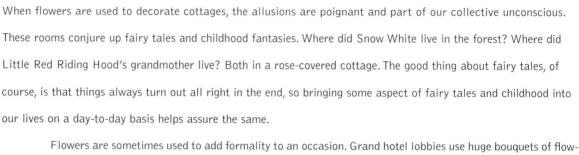

FLOWERS, LEAVES, AND GARDEN MOTIFS ARE CONSTANTS IN THE HISTORY OF DECORATION. A ROMANTIC SENSIBILITY IS WHAT DRIVES THIS LOOK.

When flowers are used to decorate cottages, the allusions are poignant and part of our collective unconscious. These rooms conjure up fairy tales and childhood fantasies. Where did Snow White live in the forest? Where did Little Red Riding Hood's grandmother live? Both in a rose-covered cottage. The good thing about fairy tales, of course, is that things always turn out all right in the end, so bringing some aspect of fairy tales and childhood into our lives on a day-to-day basis helps assure the same.

Flowers are sometimes used to add formality to an occasion. Grand hotel lobbies use huge bouquets of flowers in neoclassical urns to increase the grandeur of the experience. But in a romantic room scheme, flowers are used for just the opposite effect: to create simplicity. A wildflower bouquet, even a bunch of dandelions, picked for the dinner table by the children is far more appropriate to the overall effect of the floral cottage than a dozen long stemmed roses. Preciousness is eschewed in favor of the beauty of the ordinary. Imperfection is valuable. Folk art is emblematic of this look. Its two chief characteristics, earnestness and naiveté, are exactly what floral cottage rooms aspire to be. In this motif, hand-me-downs are far more valuable than expensive antiques.

Flowers, leaves, and garden motifs are constants in the history of decoration. A romantic sensibility is what drives this look. Opposite of the classicist, who is driven by adherence to the compositional principles of proportion, balance, and simplicity, the romanticist yearns for extravagance and sentimentality. And though motifs drawn from nature are sometimes employed in rooms with more classical tendencies—the acanthus leaves that are part of Corinthian capitals, for instance, or delicate Pompeian wall decoration—flowers are mainly in the realm of the romantic.

The desire to cover the walls with flowers goes hand in hand with a desire to be surrounded with a vintage feel: wicker chairs, hooked rugs, corroded metal, peeling paint. The whole effect is created anecdotally, in vignettes. Exceedingly casual, this look is achieved with nothing more ordered than the pattern of ornate flower arrangements on the wallpaper. Wallpaper, in this aesthetic, is universal.

Set against a floral wallpaper background, a sampler, found at a flea market, announces the arrival of spring and the inherent optimism that spring blossoms bring. Hand embroidery, as seen on the small cushion on the rocking chair as well as on the sampler, adds to the rustic, romantic feeling of this room.

It may seem natural that this look be confined to rural life, but there are many examples of urban dwelling that use floral motifs—most often as a shelter from the modern world, as a way to slow it down at home. That fol art and vintage wallpaper can be procured over the Internet and at various urban retailers points to the desirabilit of the look, regardless of the larger context. Escape is an enduring desire.

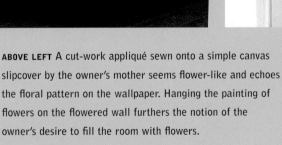

ABOVE LEFT A cut-work appliqué sewn onto a simple canvas slipcover by the owner's mother seems flower-like and echoes the floral pattern on the wallpaper. Hanging the painting of flowers on the flowered wall furthers the notion of the owner's desire to fill the room with flowers.

ABOVE RIGHT A painting by the artist Jack Pierson was inspired by a garden sign. It is the contrast between the modern, tongue-in-cheek painting and the traditional iron urn that makes this vignette poignant.

A circus carpet, actually made for one of the rings of a three-ring circus, covers most of the floor in this small bedroom. The carpet, along with the yellow framed portrait of a bouquet of flowers, the mismatched head and foot board of the bed, and the night stand painted by German artist George Grosz, create a room that at first glance seems almost naive in its sensibility. However, on closer inspection the room, through its carefully edited objects, is quite sophisticated.

OPPOSITE The owner's intense interest in modern art is not hindered by his parallel penchant for the simplicity of floral cottage. The two sentiments coexist happily.

ABOVE In the master bedroom of a Provincetown house, the owner has constructed a headboard using balusters and table legs. Set against the flowered wallpaper, it is reminiscent of a picket fence in the garden. The handmade pillow and crocheted afghan are more valuable to the owner than the finest linen bedding.

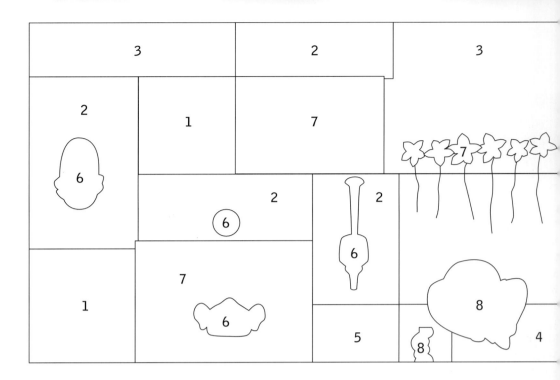

list of ingredients

flowerpower

1
Floral wallpaper
The use of floral wallpaper in this design aesthetic is essential. Floral wallpapers with overall patterns are available through most companies that produce wall covering. Patterns may be large- or small-scaled, symmetrical or random, in both traditional and nontraditional palettes. Choosing a floral wallpaper is the quickest and surest way to fill a room with flowers.

2
Gardenesque fabrics
Crewel-stitched fabrics are fabrics embroidered with a loosely twisted yarn on a linen or cotton cloth. Floral patterns are particularly popular patterns for these fabrics. They can be used not only on toss cushions, but on larger pieces of upholstery, like chairs and ottomans as well. Floral fabrics can be woven or printed. In most cases, when using more than one floral pattern in a room, vary the scale of the pattern, the size of the flower, and the ground color. Layer different floral patterns on one another—floral pillows on floral sofas against floral wallpaper sitting on floral

carpets. Bark cloth, so called because of its tree-bark-like texture, was a popular 1940's fabric. Reissued by Michelle Mancini of Full Swing the fabric is available in floral motifs and adds to the vintage feel of the floral style.

3
Flowered carpets
Hooked carpets bring just the right feel to a floral cottage. The chunky texture and nostalgic quality—when there was more time for leisure, women often made hooked carpets—exemplifies both the extravagant and the sentimental nature of this style.

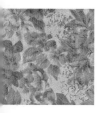

loral bedding

Pillowcases made from scraps of floral, striped, and checked quilting fabrics edged in rickrack or mbroidered ribbon are an alternative to ubiquitous white nens. These, coupled with other floral sheets and a patchwork uilt, are true to the spirit of the ustic floral interior.

7
Appliqué

Details like patchwork, embroidery, and appliqué are important ingredients in defining this floral style. Often available at flea markets, look for these techniques on bed or table linens, toss cushions, or as scraps of fabric. They go a long way in adding a romantic, nostalgic feel to a room.

ile

se a sunflower tile for a tiled abletop or as part of a kitchen acksplash. In either case, because le is often used more sparingly han fabric, the flower pattern can e much bolder.

8
Cord

Though rickrack and ribbon are the obvious trim choice, don't overlook more traditional trims. When paired with simple floral fabrics, sophisticated cords and tapes take on a naive feel.

Weathered hardware

orroded and painted metal hooks, rawer pulls, and door knockers— me with floral motifs—look like ey came from the rose covered ottages of fairy tales. A delicate rawer pull, decoupage under glass, akes for a lovely detail on a small ainted chest of drawers or night and.

romanticwhite

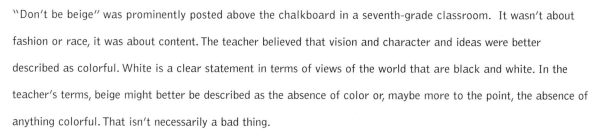

SHADES OF WHITE CAN SUGGEST SOMETHING ABOUT ESSENTIAL QUALITIES.

"Don't be beige" was prominently posted above the chalkboard in a seventh-grade classroom. It wasn't about fashion or race, it was about content. The teacher believed that vision and character and ideas were better described as colorful. White is a clear statement in terms of views of the world that are black and white. In the teacher's terms, beige might better be described as the absence of color or, maybe more to the point, the absence of anything colorful. That isn't necessarily a bad thing.

The absence of strong color can be the presence of subtlety. The meaning of beige-ness changes when it's called warm white. Making beige a cousin of white makes it more romantic. Pure white can be considered cold, unyielding. Off-white is more ambiguous, more nuanced, and more forgiving.

Shades of white can suggest something about essential qualities. Without color, one must rely on a keener visual sense. Without color, texture becomes more important, tone is described by sheen. Color in this context might be described as synthetic or unnatural. Off-white can be described as wholesome, as the absence of synthetic substances: think of whole-wheat flour.

Warm whites are often used to speak of luxury. Travertine marble, raw silk, linen, and ivory are all luxuriously off-white. And though some of the best new hotels—l'Ermitage in Los Angeles, and the W Hotel in New York, for example—are predominantly neutral, they are also contemporary. Rooms decorated with all light fabrics and finishes are, in the mind's eye, modern. But warm white also works very well in traditional rooms.

Unlike pure white, the use of off-white in rooms doesn't preclude other finishes. In rooms where warm white is the predominant color, everything else stands out. Mahogany, nickel, and pewter all work well in a warm-white environment. Warmer metal finishes—antique brass, patinated bronze, and gold leaf—work particularly well.

Often the relationship between inside and outside can be abrupt. These rooms allow varying degrees of transition. In the foreground, high windows and glass doors allow light to flood the winter garden. The light and the garden bench make the room feel like an outdoor space. The trellis beyond encloses an outdoor space, making it feel like a room.

Rooms like these are easy to create using basic materials. Traditional molding finished with shiny off-whit[e] paint is as beautiful as it is simple to do. Choose a white on white wallpaper, white canvas upholstery, open weav[e] linen curtains hanging from brass rods, Indonesian wood and cane chairs, an ebonized coffee table, and you have [a] perfect romantic white environment to begin personalizing the space with artwork and antiques. And what could b[e] a better for this warm environment than the light of a few strategically placed candles?

The small scale of the rooms in this Boston townhouse did not inspire the use of small-scale furniture. On the contrary, commodious, comfortable furniture like the wing chair and four-poster bed in the master bedroom is the standard. Simple, natural floor covering and white cotton duck used throughout the house allow the decorative elements— the carved, gold-framed mirror, the painting, and the prints—to stand out. Dark wood, which can seem heavy and traditional in some settings, looks at home in this not-quite-traditional environment.

PREVIOUS PAGE AND BELOW Deep-colored walls have a way of enveloping and unifying all the furnishings in a room. White walls have just the opposite effect. That is why most museum objects are set against white walls. A white wall bounces light and makes the objects stand out. The lesson to be learned for rooms at home is that unless the objects are as interesting an assortment as they are here—Mexican antiques, polychromed icons, a raw metal shelf, Barcelona chairs, and baroque andirons—it may be better that they not get the full attention that stark white walls might give them.

RIGHT A simple composition can say a lot. The two chairs against the chair rail are standing ready to enlarge any gathering. The six family photos with white mats and basic black frames remind the visitor of the importance of family history. The white walls lend an air of quiet elegance to the space.

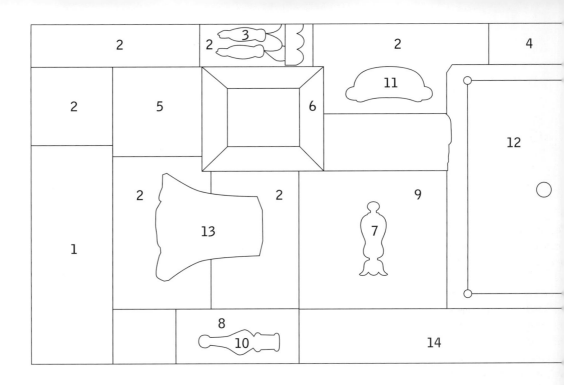

list of ingredients

1
Tibetan carpet
Traditional techniques and
materials are used to produce
luxurious hand-woven carpets. They
are generally available in either 50
or 100 knots per inch. The subtle
sheen at the edge is created by
using silk that is dyed the same
color as the wool ground.

2
Winter white fabrics
When white fabric is an important
ingredient in a room, variations
in texture and scale lend a visual
complexity. Pattern created with
stitching, like this windowpane
check, with square dots or with
brush fringe, can all be used
together. The open-weave mohair
makes an elegant throw, while the
wool boucle could cover a well-
tailored sofa.

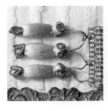

3
Tassel fringe
Curtains made of simple white
fabric become a more prominent
part of the decorative scheme with
the addition of a highly detailed
fringe. Whether used on the edge
of a silk panel, or as a contrast to
fabric with a more matte finish, the
fringe picks up light and draws the
eye to the windows.

4
Bullion fringe
When the bottom edge of a skirt
is trimmed with bullion, a sofa or
chair looks more finished.

Textured tile

Traditional white tile bathrooms, reminiscent of spas, are a perfect way to complete a white house. In the past few years, many manufacturers have gone a step beyond plain white tiles to produce interesting profiles and intricate textures. Used with nickel plated fittings and claw footed tubs, these tiles can help update a noble and luxurious tradition.

Gold frame

Whether used to frame art or family photos, the soft warmth of a gold finish works well in warm, off-white rooms. Depending on what's going inside the frame, choose a simple wide, flat, molding or an ornate carved frame that is not simply mitered at the corners, but finished with special corner moldings. Gold leaf is the best gold finish, sometimes laid over a red-orange base for a warmer burnished look; if budget is a concern, however, other painted gold finishes will work well.

7
Antique perfume bottle

The sensuous shape of this bottle makes it a perfect element in a romantic table scape.

8
Distressed painted surface

Surfaces that have a sense of history add a lot of character to a room. Antiques and found objects often have beautifully distressed finishes, but believable antique-looking finishes can be created by good craftsmen. The logic of the distressing should reflect how an old surface would have worn. For example, usually the area around a pull is more worn than the rest of the surface from years of use.

9
Broadloom carpet

Thick, white, wall-to-wall carpet evokes the kind of glamour that you see in the movies. The reflection from white floors help to fill rooms with light.

10
Finial

Decorative hardware for curtains are the kind of details that will help complete the look of a room. Window treatments offer numerous opportunities for hardware details: besides finials there are rods, brackets, and tiebacks to consider.

11
Brass bin pull

Traditional bin or scoop pulls give a cabinet a sense of history and permanence. The traits to look for when choosing a pull are that the metal feels thick enough and the lead edge that your hand comes in contact is smooth and rounded rather than a square edge.

12
Mahogany box

Using dark wood in predominantly white interiors gives rooms a sense of tradition by suggesting a colonial outpost. The mother of pearl inlay on this simple box adds the same kind of finish that nail head trim adds to a chair, or brush fringe adds to the edge of a pillow.

13
Beaded candle shade

A beaded candle shade makes the light from a candle even more romantic and the warm white in a room even warmer.

14
Striped wallpaper

Subtly patterned, almost-white wallpaper adds surface interest to plain walls without being intrusive or busy. Sets of antique prints, simply framed, look especially good on wallpaper.

classically composed

WITHIN EACH ROOM, SYMMETRY, BALANCE, AND PROPORTION ARE KEY INGREDIENTS. THE ARCHITECTURAL STRUCTURE AND CHARACTER OF THE SPACE SHOULD BE RESPECTED.

Just like in music, art, and architecture, decoration can be broadly separated into two categories: classic and romantic. Romantic rooms are sentimental and decorative while decorum, propriety, and refinement are words that describe the way classic rooms are assembled. Classic is not a style so much as it is an attitude or sensibility. If romanticism is about intuition and sentiment, classicism is about rationality and fact. Architects often use the rules of classicism when creating rooms.

A hundred years ago, with the publication of *The Decoration of Houses* by Edith Wharton and Ogden Codman. Jr., an articulate diatribe against the "vulgarity" of romantic Victorian decoration, the classic-romantic dichotomy in decoration was exposed. To classicists, romantic rooms are irrational and excessive. A hundred years later the dichotomy continues.

In a classic approach to decorating, rooms, rather than flowing spaces, are important. The current trend for great rooms that are part kitchen, part family room, and part dining room is a difficult venue to pursue this look. The whole notion of an "open plan" house—an idea embraced by the great American architect Frank Lloyd Wright—is a romantic idea centered on an idealized lifestyle. In a more classic approach, if rooms are connected, they might simply be connected with a compositional axis. For example, if three rooms are adjacent and their doors are aligned, that is called an enfilade. The rooms are connected by virtue of the lined up doorways that create an axis, but each room remains a discreet space. Each room can be decorated, furnished, and lit independently to suit the function. The group of rooms can be unified if the moldings are painted the same throughout. If the wall colors are chosen to work as a palette, all of the rooms will have a similar feel.

Within each room, symmetry, balance, and proportion are key ingredients. The architectural structure and character of the space should be respected. Pay attention to the position of windows for instance. If windows are symmetrical about the room, whatever furniture is in front of them should be symmetrical as well. Make sure the chandelier is exactly centered. Arrange seating on an axis with the fireplace. Choose a carpet that is the right shape for the room. Decorating in this manner isn't an approximate endeavor, it is exacting. The overall effect should feel

In this living room, the owner has played with the proportions of the space. Curtains are hung on a rod mounted close to the ceiling while a large painting dominates the room. These manipulations have created a room that feels larger and airier yet still well composed and inviting.

considered. Everything in the space, from wall colors to lampshades, should be part of the look. Of course that should

be the case no matter what the style of the room, but in classic rooms, it is even more so. This is not a look created

by invention and personal whimsy. There is no place for quirky objects and odd colors. These are rooms where every

thing is composed. Nothing is left to chance. These are rooms created from tasteful objects that always seem to have

an important provenance (whether or not they really do). Books are right at home here. Looking at photos of rooms

like these, you can almost hear the mantle clock ticking.

ABOVE LEFT A modern take on a classic composition includes tobacco-colored walls, a matte metal table lamp, and thin rectangular mirror. It is less about the objects themselves and more about how they are arranged that categorizes this vignette as classic design.

ABOVE RIGHT Flanking the entrance of each door are well-composed vignettes that easily lead visitors from one space to the next. By aligning doors and allowing one room to open directly onto the next, small spaces work better as part of a whole rather than as discreet entities.

By opening up three small rooms and creating this enfilade, the owner of this apartment has created spaces large enough to entertain a crowd, yet cozy enough to curl up on the sofa with a book.

ABOVE In classic decoration, pay close attention to the arrangement of things. Balance, symmetry, and proportion are key ingredients in composition. In the study, a slim table lamp and framed print offset a vase with flowers. The table on which the delicate arrangement sits is in turn part of a symmetrical arrangement.

OPPOSITE In classically composed rooms, there is very little, if anything left to chance. Furniture is carefully arranged. Objects are carefully placed. If this formula seems stiff or a bit off-putting, this house proves it doesn't have to be. The owner, an architect and designer, is sensitive to the rules of classic design but still manages to create a room that is comfortable and modern.

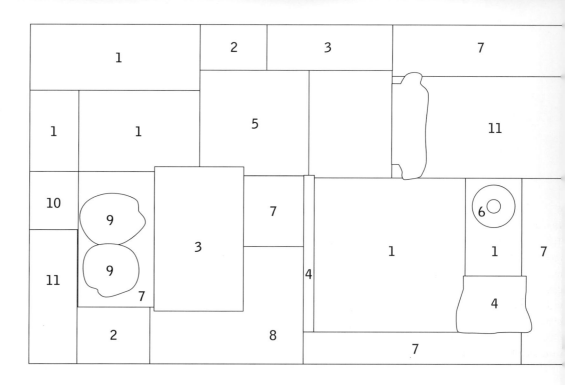

list of ingredients

classicallycomposed

1

Silk and wool

Contrasting texture not only makes a room more interesting to the touch, it makes it better looking. Fabrics reflect light differently. Nappier textures produce flat even surfaces while harder, shinier textures reflect light. Achieve a stylish look by using two fabrics that are the same color but have different surfaces, like silk and wool.

2

Synthetic suede

If you think of it as ersatz suede, it will never measure up. But as a polypropylene material unrelated to animal skin, you can't beat it. Virtually indestructible, its nappy surface and matte finish give it an elegant quality that works well in either a traditional or modern rooms. Because it takes dye well, it is produced in a myriad of colors, from bright synthetic hues to subtle mixed colors that are hard to name. The latter range is a good ingredient in a classic decor. The soft "hand" of the fabric makes it a popular choice for favorite reading chairs.

3

Seagrass mat, coir mat, sisal mat

Floors covered with natural mats were so popular in the mid 1990s that synthetic and wool versions were produced by almost every major manufacturer. But with all the best intentions and ease of maintenance (not a trait of natural floor coverings), there is nothing like the real thing. A room whose floor is covered in one of these materials is well along the way to becoming an oasis of calm. Often floors fitted with mats have other, more decorative area rugs laid over them, just as you would with a wood floor.

4
Hemp trimmings

Though produced as part of the recent trend toward nonsynthetic materials, the unique, brown-gray color of this material works well with most grayed-down palettes—often an important ingredient in classically composed rooms where vivid color is out of place.

5
Grasscloth

A wall covering that had its heyday in mid twentieth-century decoration, grasscloth is now being produced in soft, beautiful colors rather than just the natural brown color that was so popular. If cut into rectangles and the grain alternated in a checkerboard pattern, the wall becomes changeable. Like iridescent fabrics, or hand-woven carpets, the dark-light relationship of each "tile" reverses when seen from different angles. The grid created by the panels can help organize the architectural structure of a room.

6
Patinated metal

Surfaces that change with age and exposure to the elements, materials that weather, are nice to be around. Like a lined face, they seem knowing. Slick surfaces that ward off change, the kind of surface that when nicked or scratched become damaged rather than aged, also ward off warm feelings. They seem distant and standoffish. But metals that rust, copper that slowly turns green, painted surfaces that eventually leave only traces of color—these are the kinds of materials that feel like they have a past worth saving. Even shiny brass hardware will age gracefully if you remove the protective lacquer coating and allow it to slowly but surely corrode.

7
Paint palette

When the decorative scheme for a whole house is conceived, the whole palette should be considered rather than thinking about it room by room. The stair hall and corridors are, in a way, the most important. They will tie the rest of the scheme together. Painted moldings serve the same function. Although there is no hard and fast rule about the color of trim, if it is painted in a similar manner throughout the house, the shift in wall color from room to room will be more apparent and can be more subtle.

8
Slate

Though it may remind you of the chalkboard in grammar school, slate is a beautiful, durable, and reasonably inexpensive surface. This slate, quarried in Vermont, is as appropriate indoors as it is out, as functional on the kitchen counter as it is on the floor of the bathroom. It is available in gray-green, gray-purple, brick red, and black. Unlike other more porous stone, slate requires no special finish and can be cleaned with soap and water.

9
Color poms for custom carpets

Custom carpets are often a good solution for rooms that are an odd size or have a particular color scheme. Although more expensive than buying a carpet "off the rack," they may not be more than a good antique. Designing a custom carpet allows you to control the amount of color and texture that is appropriate for the room.

10
Fitted carpets

Generally referred to as wall-to-wall, broadloom carpet—the name comes from the width of the loom on which the carpet is produced—is a minimum of 12 feet wide, allowing many rooms to be fitted with very few seams. Though wall-to-wall has taken on less than classic connotations—the low point being the moment when rust-colored shag wall-to-wall carpeting was paired with brown velour sofas—it has a place in even the most classically correct rooms. Though synthetic fibers can have a disturbing sheen or sparkle, wool can be expensive. Do not choose broadloom based on a tiny swatch in a folder. When it installed in the room in a huge expanse, it will surely surprise you if you haven't looked at a larger sample. Most manufacturers will provide one so you can make a more informed decision.

11
Silver tea paper

Walls that are covered in silver paper shimmer in candlelight and sparkle in sunlight.

insideout

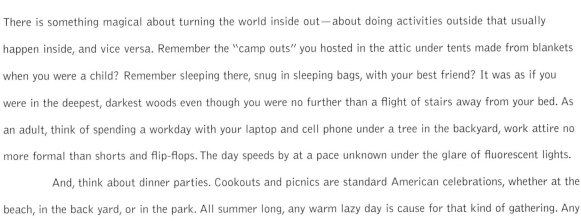

AN **OUTDOOR** ROOM CAN BE DEFINED BY WALLS:
CLIPPED HEDGES, TRELLISES, OR STONE WALLS WILL
ESTABLISH **DEFINITIVE ENCLOSURE.**

There is something magical about turning the world inside out—about doing activities outside that usually happen inside, and vice versa. Remember the "camp outs" you hosted in the attic under tents made from blankets when you were a child? Remember sleeping there, snug in sleeping bags, with your best friend? It was as if you were in the deepest, darkest woods even though you were no further than a flight of stairs away from your bed. As an adult, think of spending a workday with your laptop and cell phone under a tree in the backyard, work attire no more formal than shorts and flip-flops. The day speeds by at a pace unknown under the glare of fluorescent lights.

And, think about dinner parties. Cookouts and picnics are standard American celebrations, whether at the beach, in the back yard, or in the park. All summer long, any warm lazy day is cause for that kind of gathering. Any food that can be easily prepared over a charcoal fire is ubiquitous fare. But here is another way to dine al fresco. Imagine an elegant dinner for six. Design a creative menu. Use your best china, silver, stemware, and linen. Light the table with candles. But instead of serving dinner in the dining room, move the feast outside, to a covered porch, or trellis-enclosed roof deck.

One of the most important ingredients for turning an outdoor space into an outdoor room is furniture. A table and comfortable chairs will define a space and allow for a host of activities, from dining to board games. If the outdoor room is used during the day, the shade of an awning or an umbrella—even the shade from an adjacent building—is a necessary ingredient. The extent of an outdoor room can be marked by the perimeter of a deck or patio, or it might be implied by a border garden. An outdoor room can be defined by walls: clipped hedges, trellises, or stone walls will establish definitive enclosure. Floors can be brick, stone, wood, or grass. Outdoor rooms can be lit with lanterns or strings of party lights.

Indoor furnishings can also be brought outside during good weather for dramatic effect. Hanging candelabra from an extended tree branch will define a space with the soft glow of candlelight. In covered areas, floors can have sisal or woven plastic mats. But bringing a "good" carpet onto the lawn or patio can add an extravagant, luxurious feel to an outdoor dinner party.

Making rooms in unexpected places, in unexpected ways, takes extra planning. When choosing to turn a room inside out use imagination, take chances, and laugh with your guests when unexpected rain arrives.

Offering both privacy and a view of the garden, this lattice wall creates an outdoor room. A vintage 1940's tablecloth, ivy tableware, and terra-cotta pots filled with wheat grass make a great garden-inspired table setting indoors or out.

TOP LEFT A tour of an eighteenth-century New England town often reveals a variety of stone walls that speak to a house's permanence and history. The stone wall of this outdoor room is newly constructed and offers an intricately patterned backdrop to art.

MIDDLE LEFT An addition to a charming cottage opens onto a patio, doubling the size of the kitchen. The outdoor space is used all the time, weather permitting. It is the perfect spot to enjoy a cup of coffee and read the morning paper or have friends over for supper on a Saturday night. The French doors allow for easy movement from inside to outside.

BOTTOM LEFT Furniture that does double duty is useful for creating outdoor rooms. Here, a drop-leaf table can be set for a cozy breakfast for two or be opened up to accommodate a dinner for six. When company isn't coming, the table is used to hold plants and small gardening tools or as a work surface for an outdoor office.

OPPOSITE Archways and white stucco walls allude to tropical vacation spots. Using this porch for dining, reading, or to catch up on correspondence, makes coming home feel like a year-round holiday. The vintage white wicker chairs and iron table are the perfect foil for the stucco walls.

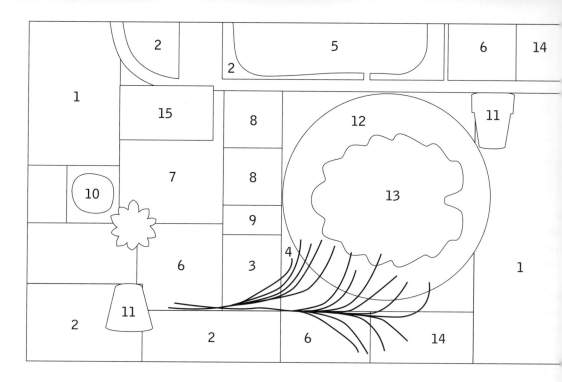

list of ingredients

1
Vintage tablecloths
When not being used for a game of canasta or mah jong, the ubiquitous folding card table of the 1950s was often covered with these. Popular again, these small tablecloths can often be found at flea markets and vintage stores. Their flower or fruit patterns make them great for garden parties.

2
Outdoor fabrics
Fabrics that can be used both indoors and outdoors are a natural choice for creating outdoor rooms. These fabrics won't fade in the sun, they're resistant to mildew, and they can be hosed down, so a sudden summer rainstorm won't affect them. Awning or ticking stripes are a natural choice.

3
Rubberized linen
Roger and Goffigon's rubberized linens are water-resistant and come in chic, natural colors. They're great for shower curtains as well.

4
Scuba diving suit fabric
Once used almost exclusively for scuba diving suits, this nylon and elastin water-repellent fabric comes in a range of colors that can now be used for very stylish upholstery.

6
Garden furniture

Garden furniture can be used indoors and outdoors. Vintage pieces, like this perforated metal garden chair, can be used around a modern dining table—if you're lucky enough to find a set intact. If there's only one piece to be had, set it against a stone or stucco garden wall to create a charming vignette.

Slate

A beautiful and durable material, slate is appropriate for both indoor and outdoor use. Use it as a "floor" for an outdoor room. Available in a range of colors from gray-green and gray-purple to brick red and black, it can be cleaned easily with soap and water. And, unlike more porous stone, slate needs no special finish.

7
Sisal

A sisal carpet bordered with a twill tape makes a great outdoor carpet. Relatively lightweight, it can be brought indoors if there's a sudden downpour.

8
Concrete tiles

If you think concrete should be restricted to a house's foundation, think again. Now available in glorious colors, concrete tiles can be used to create beautiful floors and garden walls to create outdoor rooms.

9
Molding

This wood molding was faux painted to look like aged copper. Use faux finishes for instant aging—but leave the rest to mother nature.

10
Brick flower pots

Found in an old warehouse, this 1930's square flower pot fashioned from a brick is an example of an oversupply of goods put to clever and fashionable use.

11
Belgian pot and glazed pot

Antique handmade flowerpots from Belgium are a charming addition to a picnic table or plant stand. The same goes for the green and blue glazed terra cotta pot. And the mossier the better.

12
Wicker and rattan

Wicker and rattan are a perfect choice of materials for furnishings and accessories to be used out of doors. Beside vintage pieces, which often have a lovely patina and curvy shape, look for tightly woven, naturally colored, clean-lined wicker for a more modern approach.

13
Leaf dish

From the famed Parisian florist Christian Tortu comes this palm leaf-shaped plate. Look for tableware with garden motifs to set the tone for dining al fresco.

14
Palette

When creating outdoor rooms borrow from nature. Choose the rich greens of plantings, the golden yellow of the sun, and the bluest sky blue.

15
Wheat grass

A box of wheat grass in an old crate makes a playful, whimsical centerpiece.

resourcelist

Corrugated Plastic

Excelite
104 Maple Ave.
Inglewood, Ontario LON 1KO
800-268-7410
www.grahamfrp.com

Fabrics

China Seas Inc. of Quadrille
50 Day St.
Bldg. 1, 5th Floor
Jersey City, NJ 07306

Clarence House Imports Ltd.
211 E. 58th St.
New York, NY 10022-1295
800-632-0076
www.clarencehouse.com

Designers Guild
90 Commerce St.
Stamford, CT 06902
203-359-1500

Donghia Furniture/Textiles, Ltd.
485 Broadway
New York, NY 10013-5901
800-DONGHIA
www.donghia.com

Full Swing Textiles Collection
474 Thames St.
Newport, RI 02840
www.fullswingonline.com

Henry Calvin
2046 Lars Way
Medford, OR 97501
888-732-1996
www.henrycalvin.com

Kravet Fabrics Inc.
225 Central Avenue South
Bethpage, NY 11714
888-4-KRAVET
www.kravet.com

Rogers and Goffigon
979 3rd Ave.
New York, NY 10022
212-888-3242

Scalamandre Silks Inc.
942 3rd Ave.
New York, NY 10022-2701
800-932-4361
www.scalamandre.com

Floor Covering

Cork

Expanko Cork Co. Inc.
1139 Phoenixville Pike
West Chester, PA 19380
800 345 6202
www.expanco.com

Wicanders Cork
586 Bogert Rd.
River Edge, NJ 07661
800 828 2675

Handmade Carpets

Elizabeth Eakins Inc.
21 E. 65th St.
New York, NY 10021
212-628-1950

Steven King Inc.
1 Design Center Place
Suite 405
Boston, MA 02210
617-426-3302

Paper and Sisal

Merida Meridian, Inc.
643 Summer Street
Boston, MA 02210
800-345-2200
www.sisalcarpet.com

Vinyl Tile

Forbo Industries Inc.
PO Box 667
Humboldt Industrial Park
Hazleton, PA 18201
800-842-7839
www.forbo_industries.com

Hardware

The Colonial Brass Company
511 Winsted Rd.
Torrington, CT 06790
800-355-7894
www.colonialbronze.com

Liz's Antique Hardware
453 S. La Brea Ave.
Los Angeles, CA 90036
323-939-4403
www.lahardware.com

Urban Archaeology
143 Franklin St.
New York, NY 10013
212-431-4646
www.urbanarchaeology.com

Metal

Coiled Metal

Cascade Coil Drapery
1239 SE 12th Ave.
Portland, OR 97214
800-999-COIL
www.cascadecoil.com

Perforated Metals
McNichols Co.
45 Powers Rd.
Westford, MA 01886
800-237-3820
www.mcnichols.com

Stamped Metal Ceilings

W.F. Norman Corp.
PO Box 323
Nevada, MO 64772
800-641-4038

Textured Stainless Steel

Rimex Metals
2850 Woodbridge Ave.
Edison, NJ 08837
800-526-7600
www.rimexmetals.com

Woven Metal

Howard Wire and Cloth Co.
28976 Hopkins St.
Hayward, CA 94545
800-969-3559
www.howardwire.com

Paint

Benjamin Moore
51 Chestnut Ridge Rd.
Montvale, NJ 07645
800-344-0400
www.benjaminmoore.com

Donald Kaufman Color Collection
800-977-9198
Available at:
Santa Monica Painter's Supply
1625 17th St.
Santa Monica CA 90404

The Color Factory
114 West Pallisade Ave
Englewood, NJ 07631-2692

Plastic Laminates

Abet Laminati
Abet, Inc.
100 Hollister Road
Teterboro, NJ 07608
800-228-2238

Formica
10155 Reading Rd.
Cincinatti, OH 45241
800-FORMICA
www.formica.com

Nevamar
8339 Telegraph Rd.
Odenton, MD 21113
800-638-4380
www.nevamar.com

Solid Surfacing

Dupont Corian
800-986-6444
www.corian.com

Fountainhead
8305 Telegraph rd.
Odenton, MD 21113
877-386-4323
www.ftnhead.com

Surell
10155 Reading Rd.
Cincinatti, OH 45241
800-FORMICA
www.formica.com

Stores and Catalogues

Anthropologie
1700 Sansom St.
6th Floor
Philadelphia, PA 19103
800-309-2500 (catalogue)
www.anthropologie.com

Black Ink @ Home
370 Broadway
Cambridge, MA 02139
617-576-0707

Charles River Street Antiques
45 River St.
Boston, MA 02114
617-367-3244

Craft Caravan
63 Greene St.
New York, NY 10012-4372
212-431-6669

Crate & Barrel
For the store nearest you:
800-996-9960
Catalogue: 800-323-5461
www.crateandbarrel.com

Garnet Hill Inc.
231 Main St.
Franconia, NH 03580
800-622-6216
www.garnethill.com

Home Depot Inc.
www.homedepot.com

Marie Decor
737 La Cienaga Boulevard
Los Angeles, CA 90069
310-289-0799
www.mariedecor@aol.com

Martha By Mail
P.O. Box 60060
Tampa, FL 33660-0060
800-950-7130
www.marthabymail.com

Nomad
1741 Mass Ave.
Cambridge, MA 02140-2217
617-497-6677

Pottery Barn
For a store nearest you call:
800-922-5507

Restoration Hardware
For a store nearest you call:
415-924-1005

Smith + Hawken
For a store nearest you call:
800-940-1170

Target Stores
For a store nearest you call:
800-800-8800

Waterworks
800-927-2120
www.waterworks.com

Yard Company
8430 Germantown Ave.
Philadelphia, PA 19118
215-247-3390

For a complete shopping guide
to home design stores in
Los Angeles, Boston, San
Francisco, and New York log
on to www.homeportfolio.com

Tiles

Armstrong World Industries
800-233-3823
www.armstrong.com

Rep Tiles
285 Washington Street
Somerville, MA 02143
617-628-6550
www.rep_tiles.com

Rubber Flooring

PRF USA
PO Box 6505
Carlstadt, NJ 07072
800-752-2218

Wall Covering

Elizabeth Dow, Ltd.
155 Avenue of the Americas
New York, NY 10013
212-219-8822
212-941-1331 Fax
www.elizabethdow.com

Laura Ashley Inc.
6 St. James Ave.
Boston, MA 02116
800-367-2000
www.laura-ashleyusa.com

Osborne & Little
90 Commerce Rd.
Stamford, CT 06902
203-359-1500

Sanderson
979 3rd Ave.
New York, NY 10022
212-319-7220

Wheels

Acorn Industrial Products
7 Union Hill Dr.
West Conshohocken, PA 19428
800-523-5474
www.acornindprod.com

Window Coverings

Beauti-Vue Products (which
handles Nanik Woodblinds)
8555 194th St.
Bristol, WI 53104
800-558-9431
www.beautivue.com

Smith & Noble
P. O. Box 1387
Corona, CA 92878
800-765-7776
www.smithandnoble.com

For a complete shopping guide to
home design stores in Los Angeles,
Boston, San Francisco, and New
York, log on to homeportfolio.com

photocredits

Antoine Bootz: 8-13; 18-24; 30-31; 33-35; 45; 52-53; 54 (right); 55-57;72-73; 82-87; 116-118

Hornick/Rivlin: 6; 14-15; 26-27; 36-37; 48-49; 58-59; 68-69; 78-79; 88-89; 98-99; 108-109; 120-121; 124-125; 126 (right); 128-129; 130-131; 138-139

John Lawler: 119; 126 (left)

Greg Premru: 3; 25; 32; 40-41; 43 (right); 44; 46 (bottom); 47; 54 (left); 62-67; 75-76; 102-103; 104 (left); 107

Eric Roth: 2-3; 42 (left); 43; 46 (top and middle); 77; 92-97; 112-115; 127; 136-137

Paul Whicheloe: 104 (right); 105-106

designcredits

Architects and Interior Designers

Many Thanks to the following architects and designers:

Jan Barboglio

Kelly Behun

Marc and Mary Cooper

Michael Formica

Terry Hall

Paul Magnuson

Robert Miklos,
Schwartz Silver Architects

Phillip Jude Miller, America Dural

Itzhar Patkin

Heidi Pribell

Rachel Reid, Reid Design

Lloyd Schwan

Hunt Slonem

Judyth Van Amringe

Peter Wheeler,
PJ Wheeler Associates

about**the**authors

Cheryl and Jeffrey Katz are the design columnists for the *Boston Globe Magazine* and contributing editors to *American Homestyle and Gardening* magazine. They started their design company, C&J Katz Studio, in 1984. The Boston based design "think tank" is engaged in a broad range of work including retail spaces, corporate headquarters, restaurants, residences, exhibits, and furniture. C&J Katz Studio has been published extensively. Their work has appeared in *Metropolitan Home, House Beautiful, Garden Design*, and *Interior Design*. Cheryl and Jeffrey Katz have apppeared on *This Old House* for their work on the Milton project. The couple lives in Boston with their two children, Fanny and Oliver.

acknowledgments

While writing this book, we have been lucky enough to be surrounded with family, friends and colleagues who have been supportive, helpful, patient and knowledgeable. We thank them all. We would especially like to mention:

Martha Wetherill, Acquisitions Editor at Rockport Publishers for her calm manner and unwavering support and Silke Braun, Creative Director at Rockport Publishers for sharing our vision.

Kristen Wainwright, our literary agent and friend, whose level head, honesty and sense of humor guided us through this project.

The editorial staff at *The Boston Globe Magazine* who continue to encourage our belief that design ideas should be accessible.

The many people at The Boston Design Center who opened up their showrooms and allowed us to borrow whatever we needed at a moments notice to create the style boards for this book. A special thanks to the staff at Steven King Carpets, Ostrer House and Billie Brenner Ltd.

Many thanks to Deb Coburn of Nomad and Susan and Tim Corcoran of Black Ink @ Home for their creativity and support.

Thank you to our beloved studio staff, especially Kevin Musumano, Tracy Parkinson and Honah Lee Milne.

The photographers whose vision of how we look at interiors helped shape this book, and especially, Rick Hornick and Sandy Rivlin who are not only great photographers, but great friends as well.

And finally, our children, Fanny and Oliver, who endured many late night take-in dinners while we hurried to meet our deadline. Their pure, clear vision of the world is our constant inspiration.